T0329219

Cambridge Elements ☰

Elements in Religion and Violence
edited by
James R. Lewis
University of Tromsø
Margo Kitts
Hawai'i Pacific University

GREAT WAR, RELIGIOUS DIMENSIONS

Bobby Wintermute
Queens College, City University of New York

CAMBRIDGE
UNIVERSITY PRESS

CAMBRIDGE
UNIVERSITY PRESS

University Printing House, Cambridge CB2 8BS, United Kingdom

One Liberty Plaza, 20th Floor, New York, NY 10006, USA

477 Williamstown Road, Port Melbourne, VIC 3207, Australia

314–321, 3rd Floor, Plot 3, Splendor Forum, Jasola District Centre,
New Delhi – 110025, India

79 Anson Road, #06–04/06, Singapore 079906

Cambridge University Press is part of the University of Cambridge.

It furthers the University's mission by disseminating knowledge in the pursuit of
education, learning, and research at the highest international levels of excellence.

www.cambridge.org
Information on this title: www.cambridge.org/9781108712668
DOI: 10.1017/9781108670661

First published 2020

A catalogue record for this publication is available from the British Library.

ISBN 978-1-108-71266-8 Paperback
ISSN 2397-9496 (online)
ISSN 2514-3786 (print)

Great War, Religious Dimensions

Elements in Religion and Violence

DOI: 10.1017/9781108670661
Firstpublishedonline: November 2020

Bobby Wintermute

Queens College, City University of New York

Author for correspondence: Stefania Barca, sbarca68@gmail.com

ABSTRACT: The First World War was a transformative event, affecting international culture, economics, and geopolitics. Though often presented as the moment heralding a new secular era of modernity, in actuality the war experience was grounded in religious faith and ritual for many participants. This Element examines how religion was employed by the state to solicit support and civic participation, while also being subordinated to the strategic and operational demands of the combatant armies. Even as religion was employed to express dissent, it was also used as a coercive tool to ensure compliance with the wartime demands of the state on civilians.

KEYWORDS: Religion, World War I, Faith, Grief, Memory

ISBNs:9781108712668 (PB), 9781108670661 (OC)
ISSNs: 2397-9496 (online), 2514-3786 (print)

Contents

1 Religion and the State

How did the First World War reflect the spiritual and religious sensibilities of individual citizens and their larger societies? To many observers, the war simply overwhelmed faith in religion. The meat-grinder of the trenches, the escalation of destructive power wielded by armies, the strident dehumanization of the enemy: all combined to erode individual trust in God and religion. In their place, materialist secularism became the defining creed of Western society. Having lost their faith in the divine, Europeans – and to a lesser degree Americans – began to look toward themselves for inspiration. By 1930, memoirists, poets, novelists, and early historians crafted a consensus narrative of the 1914–18 war that hinged upon the dual premises of tragic incompetence and mass insanity. The mass slaughter of the Great War, they argued (from an almost uniquely Western Front perspective, it should be noted), was the result of bungled military planning and cowardly political leadership. It was the signal tragedy that should never have occurred, but which was much needed. Without the war and its tremendous loss of life and capital, the old order would have lingered well into the twentieth century, constraining the advent of modern sensibility and the triumph of secular values over tradition.

Just as with its political and social outcomes, the war's long-term effects on religion and faith are still unfolding. Catholicism underwent a dynamic shift in focus, completing its transition from a politically and socially reactionary outlook to one that became at least equally concerned with social reform. Within Protestant denominations, doctrinal splits that began in wartime still exert their influence. First articulated in 1915, Fundamentalism has not only continued to define a commitment to a literal interpretation of scriptural eschatology, it has also grown to exert tremendous political influence and power in the United States and other countries. Meanwhile the pacifist message embodied within the Society of Friends (Quakers), Mennonite, and other nonconformist denominations has continued to vie with other, more statist-oriented outlooks that embrace military conflict as part of a larger divine plan. Russian Orthodoxy is again influential and significant in its home country, rivalling and exceeding in some ways its status under the last Tsar.

The war also undermined the influence of the Ottoman Empire. Postwar settlements dissolved the Ottoman Caliphate, dividing many provinces that had been under Islamic rule since the seventh century into mandates and colonies under the control of Western European Christian empires. The fragmented political landscape that even today challenges attempts to craft stability and peace is the direct product of the end of the First World War. Judaism was also greatly affected by the First World War. Zionism acquired greater legitimacy as a viable political and social concept during the war. The 1917 Balfour Declaration signaled tacit British support for the Zionist project, signaling to Jews across the world that a Palestinian homeland was possible. Alternatively, despite their participation and sacrifices, the Jewish community of Europe was unjustly associated with shirkerism, war profiteering, and political betrayals in a new anti-Semitism that portended sinister implications.

The speed with which the churches embraced the war is remarkable, but it should not be a surprise. Over the previous century, as the Great Powers embarked on their own imperial enterprises, churches were encouraged to join the state in promoting a patriotic and nationalistic creed that validated a more strenuous foreign policy. Catholic bishops, priests, and lay ministers, for example, adopted pro-imperialist rhetoric in the late nineteenth century primarily to mark out their congregations' place alongside other groups as loyal supporters of the state. In doing so, they made a choice between the modernist humanism that was changing the face of Roman Catholicism under Pope Leo XIII and the more materialistic demands of the Church as an institution. However important intellectual and moralistic dialogue was to advancing the Catholic creed, the immediate compromises demanded by local society to preserve Church autonomy were paramount. If the state demanded accommodation with imperialist projects, then the Church was obligated to support these lest it surrender its privilege.

The focus of this section is on the interactions between organized religions and the major combatant states. Each of the primary faiths – Catholicism, Protestantism, Judaism, Eastern Orthodoxy, and Islam – is given its own section, with a last section dedicated to the Allied colonial armies. Within each section, the experiences of specific nations are discussed in detail. As the diversity of each major denomination and their subordinate case studies is presented, so too are shared characteristics that reveal how religion was a central factor in expressing national identity before, during, and after the war.

The First World War and Catholicism

The most active organized mass resistance to the war should have occurred within the Roman Catholic Church. The opening of the war was alleged to have sent Pope Pius X to his deathbed on August 20, 1914. His replacement, Benedict XV, spoke out repeatedly against the war, and ultimately declared the Church's neutrality in November 1914. He next offered to negotiate a December 1914 truce, followed by a proposed peace conference. No one took this offer seriously, which weighed heavily on Benedict throughout the war. The pope's objections to the war continued as the conflict wore on. In 1915 he was a staunch opponent to Italian intervention, citing the damage it might cause the church and its reputation. Throughout the war he attempted (unsuccessfully) to limit both sides from adopting religious symbols and themes in the name of the war effort.[1] In August 1917, he again proposed a cease fire, followed by disarmament and reconstruction. By this point, all Western participants were committed to seeing the conflict to the bitter end.

Benedict's calls for peace also went unheeded by many of his own subordinate cardinals and clergy. Nationalist war fervor proved too enticing and inclusive for church leaders in Germany, France, Belgium, Italy, and Austria-Hungary where bishops and cardinals alike rejected his peace appeals. Political expediency played a large part in these decisions. As the war drew on, the Catholic hierarchy in the combatant nations became even more belligerent, rejecting out of hand any attempts from the Vatican to broker peace. In Britain, where Catholicism was a minority faith, prelates reasoned any conduct short of total support would undercut recent political

---

[1] Adrian Gregory, "Beliefs and Religion," in Jay Winter (editor), *The Cambridge History of the First World War* (Cambridge University Press, 2014), 418–444, here 429–430.

concessions that legitimized the Church. France, though a majority Catholic nation, was coming off of decades of bitter infighting between secularist Republicans and conservative-leaning anti-Republican Catholics who sought a greater role for the Church in daily affairs. Here the majority of priests sought to prove their patriotism by supporting the war even as it was bleeding their congregations dry. German Catholics were likewise eager to win legitimacy in the eyes of the Wilhelmine court. Since the bruising contest with Prime Minister Otto von Bismarck during the *kulturkampf* of the 1870s, lingering antipathy toward Catholics in official and informal German society remained a pressing concern.[2]

There were signs, however, of greater support for Benedict XV's appeal to peace among the Catholic laity. Most noteworthy was the acclaimed miracle at the Portuguese village Fátima in May 1917. Since Portugal had joined the Allies in 1916, tensions in the rural countryside grew as the first units were sent to the Western Front. Like other Catholic majority nations, Portugal struggled even before the war with a see-saw fight for influence between urban liberals and rural conservatives – the latter enlisting the Church to win the support of pious peasants. After a group of children reported a visitation from the Archangel Michael and Virgin Mary in a grotto near Fátima, thousands of Portuguese adults seized on the event as a signal of imminent divine intervention. News of the supernatural visitations spread rapidly through the Catholic world and was interpreted in varied ways. Most observers were quick to dismiss the entire affair as the product of rural teenagers' overactive imaginations. The faithful, however, took the reports more seriously, particularly after the October 13, 1917 mass gathering in anticipation of a sixth visitation. Thousands of onlookers – skeptics and believers – saw the sun behave erratically in the sky above the site, giving weight to the arguments of those who put stock in the prophecies. Was the intervention described during the visions an end to the war, or did it represent something more total and complete? In addition to the eschatological implications of the message, some would argue the prophecies anticipated the imminent Bolshevik revolution in Russia.

[2] Ashley Beck, *Benedict XV and World War I* (Catholic Truth Society, 2007), 24–25, 37–38.

In the end, most Catholics across Europe and America supported the war. From the onset, a spiritual dialogue engaged Catholics in uniform as to the inner morality of war and its effect on the faithful. Soldiers experienced many forms of conversion and epiphany in the trenches, making combat a moral test as well as an opportunity to proselytize on behalf of the Church.[3] Similarly, the war transformed victims of the bloodshed, both soldiers and civilians, into martyrs for their faith. More than simply proof against the aggression of the enemy, their deaths demonstrated the power of the individual will to make a lonely stand against the secularism and materialism of the age. Another aspect of the interaction between the Catholic faithful and the war is its dual message of punishment and hope. Modernity had multiplied man's sins, to the point where the war was brought about – not by human agency, but by spiritual intervention – as a form of retribution. This divine sanction was not offered in isolation, however. The grief brought with it the opportunity for reconciliation with God: "In their spiritual dereliction, the combatants and their families turned to the intercession of those who could bring them temporal comfort in the face of war; the urgent needs of this calamitous time led directly to the core Christian message of sacrifice and resurrection."[4]

France

The war provoked a series of crises within churches in all countries, most notably in France. The Third Republic was avowedly secular, if not anticlerical. Its leaders sought to contain the influence of what had at times been a decidedly reactionary conservative Catholic Church through legislation and social sanction since the 1880s. Some of the charges and actions smack today of conspiracy theory, including claims that because Catholics acknowledged the Papacy as the spiritual head of their faith, they were as a whole untrustworthy and anti-French. Other claims, however, were calculated in response to the perceived threat to the secular state the

---

[3] Stéphane Audoin-Rouzeau and Annette Becker, *14–18: Understanding the Great War* (Hill and Wang, 2000, 2002), 127.

[4] *Ibid.*, 129.

Church historically presented. Since the French Revolution, Church and state were consistently at odds in France. Catholicism's stance against the First Republic, its record as a counterrevolutionary force that stood alongside the monarchy, and its perceived influence over landless peasants and impoverished workers amidst the rising power of Socialist unions and political parties gave weight to these charges. France and the Vatican ended all diplomatic relations in July 1904, opening new tensions between the Republic and the Church. As France entered the First World War, the government's relationship with the Catholic Church was at best frosty, if not openly hostile.[5]

Within the military's hierarchy, Catholics found a home. The three pillars of French conservatism were traditionally monarchists, the Church, and the military. After 1871, leftists increasingly questioned the army's loyalty to the Republic. The possibility of a new Bonaparte-style figure was never far from civilian politicians' minds. The political machinations of the erstwhile Minister of War General Georges Boulanger in the late 1880s, and accusations that he was conspiring with monarchists to install himself as a new dictator, fed this distrust. The anti-Semitic Dreyfus Affair likewise brought attention to intersections between the Catholic Right and like-minded army officers. After Captain Dreyfus's 1899 pardon, Republicans sought to bring the army to heel by breaking up what was seen as a dangerous Catholic anti-Republican clique in the officer corps. A staunch Republican supporter, General Louis André, was appointed Minister of War. He immediately purged the army's openly Catholic officers, forcing those who remained to demonstrate their loyalty by participating in the census of church property following the December 9, 1905 law ordering the separation of church and state. For their part, army officers were caught in a terrible bind, since Pope Pius X ordered all French Catholics to resist the policy.[6] By 1914, the anti-Catholic policies within the

---

[5] James F. McMillan, "French Catholics: *Rumeurs Infâmes* and the *Union Sacrée*, 1914–1918," in Frans Coetzee and Marilyn Shevin-Coetzee, *Authority, Identity and the Social History of the Great War* (Berghahn Books, 1995), 113–132, here 114.

[6] Leonard V. Smith, Stéphane Audoin-Rouzeau, Annette Becker, *France and the Great War, 1914–1918* (Cambridge University Press, 2003), 18.

army had effectively stunted the institution's professional growth. Promising young officers were denied promotion or appointment purely on the basis of their professed faith. A culture of informants permeated the army, with the war ministry spying on their own officers, and encouraging others to report on their peers suspected of being secret Catholics.[7]

For France, the war quickly became an existential crisis. With nearly one-quarter of French soil under enemy control, including some of its most productive industrial areas, as well as very fertile farmland, it was imperative that all available resources were marshalled to win the war. In this vein, the Poincaré Government oversaw a delicate truce with the French Catholic hierarchy. For the sake of the Republic, a rapprochement between the two powers was undertaken to rally the church behind the state in a *Union sacrée* to resist the German enemy to the last. Nevertheless, anticlerical politicians and editors remained skeptical of the Church's commitment to the cause. Pope Benedict XV's peace platform was greeted with open derision by the majority of French citizens, including devout Catholics. France had been violated by a rapacious and greedy neighbor for the second time in half a century, critics argued. This reasoning certainly prompted the rejection of Benedict's peace encyclical by the majority of French Catholic bishops.[8] High-ranking French clergymen took to the ecumenical pulpit and the secular stage to reject the Pope's peace initiatives, claiming the threat was too great and that Benedict, despite his best intentions, was misinformed. Anticlericals took this a step further, reading into the Pope's diplomacy an anti-French agenda. Active skeptics argued the pope's peace plans revealed his anti-French/pro-German bias. Benedict XV's peace plans were reimagined as evidence of a larger Catholic plot to exploit the war to facilitate a religious revival among the frightened masses, secretly accumulate power through the management of wartime charities, and ultimately overthrow the secular regime and replace it with a new government that was loyal to the directives of Rome. Such scurrilous rumors were hard to tamp down, and despite censorship efforts, continued to appear in leftist-leaning papers and

---

[7] Jack Snyder, *The Ideology of the Offensive: Military Decision Making and the Disasters of 1914* (Cornell University Press, 1984), 52, 73–74.

[8] *Ibid.*, 119–120.

journals until the end of the war. The charges were imaginary, but the circumstances of the Catholic Church's transnational political identity structure only fueled the rumors.[9]

The collective weight of the anticlerical rumors was significant, but ultimately they failed to diminish the wartime relationship between the Church and the Republic. In addition to the 1,500 commissioned military chaplains who served directly in the army, over 31,000 priests, monks, and seminary students entered service as soldiers and officers of the line or in the medical services. Priests regularly delivered sermons calling on congregants to give whatever they could spare to help pay for the war. Catholic hospitals took the lead in caring for wounded soldiers.[10] Such efforts were reciprocated by the Republic. Historical examples of French martial Catholicism were introduced to promote the war effort. Before the war a politically divisive symbol associated exclusively with Catholicism and the political right, Jeanne d'Arc received a makeover as an explicit depiction of French victimhood at the hand of foreign (now German) invaders and the people's patriotic stand on her behalf. Appearing in her peasant dress, she became a study in martyrdom (despite the Church's own role in her execution), a symbol of the desperate French refugee compelled to flee the despoliation of their home. Alternatively portrayed in the panoply of knighthood, Jeanne d'Arc was the martial sister-in-imagination of Marianne, an avenging icon of the French people seeking retribution against a perfidious and rapacious enemy. As Hew Strachan notes, "Both images carried patriotic overtones, even if [the first] was of a revolutionary France rather than a royalist one. The outbreak of the war, and particularly the bombardment of Reims cathedral, where Charles VII had been crowned under a standard held aloft by Joan, permitted these divergent interpretations to be integrated."[11]

[9]   McMillan, "French Catholics," 121–127.

[10] Annette Becker, *War and Faith: The Religious Imagination in France, 1914–1930* (Berg, 1998), 32–34.

[11] Hew Strachan, *The First World War, Volume I: To Arms* (Oxford University Press, 2001), 1118.

On the whole, the Catholic Church benefited from its support of the war. The French hierarchy wanted to restore the Church's place in the Republic, and to end its long status as a pariah in politics and society. There was more at stake, however, than recovering lost reputation. Theologian A. J. Hoover describes a social construct he labels as "Christian nationalism." Accordingly, the state exists not only as an ethnic or political entity based on self-determination, but also as a reflection of the people's relationship with God's plan. He writes, "If a nation is a divine creation, it follows logically that the collective mind or soul of a related ethnic group could be called a *Volksgeist*, a national spirit or soul. This spirit is something divine and essentially moral."[12] By demonstrating their own selfless commitment to the Republic, French Catholics were acknowledging their subordinate status in the relationship between church and state. The question of whether or not to accept the primacy of the secular state was moot. The Church was showing its own unwavering support for the concept of France as a Christian nation, and in the process cementing its place as an essential institution in the living, vital Republic.

Italy

After the *Risorgimento*, anticlerical sentiment dominated liberal intellectual and commerce-minded elites, particularly those from northern Italy. Lingering resentments toward the Vatican's long resistance to unification were realized in a series of public recriminations and displays that continued throughout the war. Similarly trade unionists, many of them socialists in fact or by association, looked at the Church as an oppressive institution, just one of a set of property holders that exerted their power over the workers. Conversely, rural Italian peasants remained devout and loyal to the Church, accepting its moral and social direction with little complaint. Caught between disdain and deference, Italy joined the war as a nation and community divided.[13]

---

[12] A. J. Hoover, *God, Germany, and Britain in the Great War* (Praeger Publishers, 1989), 86.

[13] R. J. B. Bosworth, *Mussolini's Italy: Life Under the Fascist Dictatorship, 1915–1945* (Penguin Books, 2005), 15, 31, 54.

Despite the concerns expressed by Pope Benedict XV, the Italian Catholic Church openly supported the war. Seizing upon the opportunity to speak to the nation at large, the Church hierarchy used the war as a metaphor for the challenges it faced as an institution in the post-*Risorgimento* age. The war was both a divine punishment and a chance for personal and communal redemption. Great suffering would follow, but by the time Italy joined the war, there was little question about what was to be expected. But the immediate pain and loss in combat would reaffirm Italian virtue, introducing a new society that would embrace the Church and its moral direction.[14]

Just as in France, Catholic clergymen and bishops also perceived the war as an opportunity for repairing the rifts between Church and society unleashed a generation before. Barred since 1865 from providing chaplains to the army, in June 1915 the Vatican appointed a bishop to the Front after the army's commander, Marshal Luigi Cadorna, proposed assigning one to each regiment. Ultimately 24,000 priests would accompany the army to the Isonzo. Military service instilled a new martial inspiration for some of the chaplains, nationalizing their outlook and paving the way for their own political conversion experience as Fascism evolved after the war. Convinced that the path to salvation resided in the hearts of men willing to embrace death for the greater good, these martial clerics transferred their disdain to pacifists, anarchists, and socialists.[15]

A more immediate dilemma, shared across ranks in the wartime Italian army, related to combat itself. Historian Vanda Wilcox describes how conscripts confronted near-existential anxiety over the prospect of killing white Catholic Europeans. She cites the perspective of one soldier in particular:

> What is the function of a soldier? To kill... Killing is a crime: up until yesterday that's what they taught us at school, in church, in our families... The penal code is pitiless with murderers ... but now instead they teach me ... that as soon as another man who they call my

[14] John Gooch, *The Italian Army and the First World War* (Cambridge University Press, 2014), 163–164.

[15] Bosworth, *Mussolini's Italy*, 88–89.

'superior' orders me to kill, I have to kill without pity or reason. When were they lying? Yesterday or today? Or maybe today and yesterday? I don't know.[16]

Expressions of this ambiguity toward the war persisted as the slaughter on the stalled Isonzo Front continued through the fall of 1917. Devout rural Catholics joined forces with urban socialists to publicly urge the government to seek peace, arguing the war had steered the nation away from prosperity. Instead, the corruption and immorality attending the war at home, and the senseless killing in the trenches, set Italy on a path toward self-destruction. Whereas at the start of 1915 the Italian Church establishment ignored Benedict XV's admonishments against the war, over two years of stalemate and static warfare had unraveled the general commitment to a cause that was never clearly defined. In the end, the laity expressed greater reservations over the moral cost of the war than the clergy, unravelling the trust many Catholics held for the Church establishment.[17]

The growing pacifist sentiment among Catholics only fueled the anger of anticlericalists. Protofascists and future *squadristi* like Roberto Farinacci targeted anti-war speakers and parliament deputies in speeches, essays, and even outright violence, decrying their pacifism as treason. Dismissed even by their uniformed coreligionists, Catholic pacifist priests were regularly chastised for abandoning their nation and their congregations by casting their lot with internal wreckers and external enemies. In this way the war effectively split the Catholic Church in Italy, undermining both its autonomy as a counterweight to the secular establishment and its legitimate authority as a moral voice for the people. As the Fascist totalitarianism of the 1920s took hold, the Church would be so divided between quiet opponents and vocal supporters of the new order that it would become a hapless and powerless bystander to Italy's descent.[18]

---

[16] Bruno Misefari, *DIario di un disertore: un anarchico contro la guerra* (Camerano Ancona: Gwynplaine, 2010), 31, quoted in Vanda Wilcox, *Morale and the Italian Army during the First World War* (Cambridge University Press, 2016), 125.

[17] Wilcox, *Morale and the Italian Army*, 146.

[18] Bosworth, *Mussolini's Italy*, 87–90.

Germany

At the start of the war, German Catholics were outnumbered nearly two to one by Protestants: twenty-four million Catholics, largely resident in southern and western Germany, as compared with forty million Lutherans and other Protestant adherents. Accordingly, Catholicism in Germany was a minority religion, not only statistically, but in terms of power and influence. With the inauguration of the German Empire in 1871, the Lutheran Church was elevated to the status of official state religion. In principle considered first among equals, the Lutheran establishment was quick to target the Catholic Church as an anti-German institution that owed more loyalty to external powers than it did to the Prussian Hohenzollern dynasty. This anti-Catholic baiting was nothing new. German dioceses had long struggled against secularization in the Rhineland. Another avenue of criticism lay in the Church's overall anti-unification position in the 1848 revolution. Most German Catholics favored a decentralized regional system that would preserve local rights and prerogatives. When the National Assembly favored a *Kleindeutsch* solution – German unification exclusive of Austria – the Church instead aligned with the reactionaries. In the wars of unification, the Church resisted Prussian attempts to lead the German states against Austria (1866) and France (1870). With unification virtually guaranteed, the Church finally conceded to the inevitability of a German state by forming the Catholic Center Party to defend its interests in the new *Reichstag*.

Anti-Catholic policies and intolerance accelerated in the 1870s. Germany's first chancellor, Otto von Bismarck, initiated a series of policies intended to curb Catholic influence that were collectively labeled the *Kulturkampf*. Between 1871 and 1876, laws were introduced in Prussia and in the German *Reichstag* restricting speech critical of the state from the pulpit, eliminating diocese schools, banning Jesuits and other related orders, limiting ecclesiastical power in the civic public sphere, and otherwise restricting the state support of bishops and other Church figures. By the mid-1870s, the strident anti-Catholic tone in domestic policy began to wane. The successful resistance mounted by the *Zentrum* (Catholic Center) Party, combined with the rise of a national and regional Catholic press committed to introducing a transnational context to the news of the repression target-ing their community, created a strong political identity to defend their status in the Second Reich. The social and political restrictions of the *Kulturkampf* unwound toward the end of the nineteenth century, but mutual suspicion between the two religions remained.[19]

An example of this suspicion is a German variation on the "infamous rumor" following French Catholics. The German version accused Catholics of being more loyal to Pope Benedict XV – the "French pope" according to General Erich Ludendorff – than the German state. These stories not only spoke to the historical memory of Church opposition to earlier unification efforts, they also fueled Lutheran anxieties over the old competition for influence and status within the German states. Adding to the suspicion was the belief in some circles that, on the basis of their faith, German Catholics, having more in common with their French and Belgian confessional partners, were more likely to sympathize with their coreligio-nists than their Protestant neighbors and Emperor. The immediate response to the suspicions levelled at German Catholics was the open split with Rome over the war. Catholic prelates were compelled to offer more vocal support for the war in their liturgies.[20]

Once the question of unequivocal support for the empire was settled, the issue remained of how to express solidarity and common cause with war. In this regard, the Catholic hierarchy followed the example of Lutheran church leaders, who were far more overt advocates of the subordination of the church to the will of the state. Catholic bishops crafted a wartime theology rooted in just war theory, noting that the conflict was initiated by a savage act of regicide, an affront to God and an action that demanded justice. Likewise the war's spread beyond the Balkans was laid at the feet of the Entente nations, casting the alliance's mobilization as a disproportionate

---

[19] Patrick J. Houlihan, *Catholicism and the Great War: Religion and Everyday Life in Germany and Austria-Hungary, 1914–1922* (Cambridge University Press, 2015), 30–31.

[20] McMillan, "French Catholics," 113–132; Elizabeth A. Foster, *Faith in Empire: Religion, Politics, and Colonial Rule in French Senegal, 1880–1940* (Stanford University Press, 2013), 100; Houlihan, *Catholicism and the Great War*, 8–9.

response to a regional crisis. Germany was thus the victim of an unholy alliance capitalizing upon the actions of Serbia. The ensuing war theology was intended to reconcile the immediate execution of state-ordered destructive and lethal force against other people and property. Given the rising extreme tone of propaganda and wartime rhetoric on both sides, it is unsurprising that the tenor of the bishops' messages of support grew extreme. Clerics not only blessed soldiers marching off to the train stations, they were direct participants in the war of words. Priests blessed artillery pieces, rifles, machine guns, and even poison gas shells. The wartime slaughter was sanctioned. Combat, and the killing associated with it, became a test of spiritual endurance for the German soldier, a divine challenge that would prove their moral worth before God.[21]

As the war continued, the stalwart support of Catholics wavered but never broke. At times, their moral qualms gave rise to direct public statements of qualified support for the war. This became particularly acute as Catholics sought to combat accusations of German atrocities. Catholic priests and intellectuals led the way in framing memoranda and manifestos rejecting Allied claims of misconduct in Belgium and Russia.[22] From 1916 forward, the *Zentrum* Party increasingly joined with Progressives and Social Democrats to challenge the harsh war aims sought by conservative Pan-Germanists in the *Reichstag*. Center leader Matthias Erzberger spoke for Catholics across Germany in rejecting annexations and harsh reparations both as running counter to the just war ideology that justified the war and as an affront to the Christian principles of his party.[23]

Austria-Hungary

Unlike Germany, Catholics in Austria-Hungary were the favored majority, making up 79 percent of all subjects in the Habsburg Empire. As the continental reach of the Habsburg Empire receded in the eighteenth and nineteenth centuries, its Austrian center extended its reach into Central

---

[21] *Ibid.*, 56–57.

[22] David Welch, *Germany, Propaganda and Total War, 1914–1918* (Rutgers University Press, 2000), 62.

[23] *Ibid.*, 181.

Europe. This process served two ends. It expanded the influence of the crown and the church into areas long lost to Christendom in the face of Ottoman expansion, but at the same time, it increased tensions with new neighbors along the pale with Eastern Orthodoxy. More so than Germany, the Austro-Hungarian Empire shared a borderlands region with multiple religious communities: Eastern and Russian Orthodox, Muslim, and Jewish communities all residing astride a dynamic border rife with tensions.

Within the empire, Catholicism was a unifying agent that helped bind together an ethnically and linguistically polyglot people. The Catholic hierarchy enjoyed tremendous advantages as the majority and traditional faith within the Habsburg lands. This privilege also came with the expectation that local and regional clerics would advocate for the primacy of the German-speaking royal family and the order the Emperor, Franz Josef, expected. Even as ethnically focused Catholicism took shape across the empire, with individual liturgies for Polish, Croatian, Slovenian, Italian, German, Hungarian, and Bohemian congregations leading the way toward individual churches, these different nationalistic-oriented faiths were bound by the universalist qualities of their shared faith. For nearly a century, historians have identified the Austro-Hungarian empire as the "sick man of Europe," an old-school autocracy doomed to collapse on account of the multiethnic diversity of its regional nationalities, which acted together as a centripetal force pulling the Habsburg Empire apart. Overlooked, however, is the role played by the Catholic Church as a centrifugal force constraining division and imparting a unifying impulse that transcended national identification. During the coming war, the Church not only unified Austrians, it sustained the faltering empire after military defeat, the November 21, 1916 death of Franz Josef, and the more immediate pressures of a three-front war.[24]

In the end total defeat proved too great to ignore, but then it also bespoke the eschatological-based outlook that was growing within the Habsburg Catholic community for some years. For premillenarian Catholics, the war was no great surprise. The press of nationalist ideologies, the growing social divides between rich and poor, the influence of

[24] Houlihan, *Catholicism and the Great War*, 24–25.

modernism and the associated widespread publication of Protestant scriptural critique: all pointed toward an imminent judgment that would sweep away the sins of hubris and temptation associated with the secularist worldview that drove contemporary Western society. The June 28, 1914 assassination of the Archduke Franz Ferdinand and his wife, Sophie, Duchess of Hohenberg, was a great yet tragic test of resolve for the faithful residing within the Habsburg Empire. Rather than becoming a signal break with the world that existed before 1914 and which came after 1918, the war represented a continuity in culture and history that had sustained a Catholicism through constant setback and confrontation over the nineteenth century. The war thus constitutes a revival of sorts for the Catholic faiths of Central Europe, even as the tide of war would ultimately turn against their secular-based national foundations. Patrick J. Houlihan credits this outlook to the nature of the Habsburg Empire itself. "While exploring new issues raised by the war," he writes, "ordinary Catholic men and women understood the conflict in terms of their traditional worldviews, adapted to new conditions."[25] Viewed in this light, the war and its outcome for Austria-Hungary – the division of the empire into a collection of smaller nations – was a great tragedy, but was also not as unsettling for the many peoples directly affected as defeat was for German Catholics. The transnational qualities of Austro-Hungarian Catholicism were better able to absorb the shock of defeat, even as it had also sustained unity in peace.

Great Britain

Despite winning acceptance as a legitimate faith in the 1829 Roman Catholic Relief Act, the established Church kept a low profile in public life through the nineteenth century in England. Cognizant of its minority status, the Church generally deferred in the larger arena of public advocacy and policy outside of its advocacy for Catholic schools and health care systems for their own communities. Throughout the war, the bishops in Great Britain aligned themselves firmly on the side of the government and the war effort, rejecting papal peace initiatives as needless meddling in the secular affairs of the participants. The Archbishop of Westminster, Francis Cardinal Bourne,

[25] *Ibid.*, 51.

would appeal directly to Benedict XV asking him not to anger Whitehall through his constant appeals to peace, lest the British people and government both turn their anger against Catholics.

The ecumenical context of the British Catholic bishops' rejection of Benedict XV's call to peace was founded upon the application of just war theory to the conflict and to its proposed resolution. Crafted over centuries to reconcile statist violence with personal religious conviction, at the heart of just war theory was the argument that if undertaken for select purpose, war was not an immoral act. Philosophically it is intended to reconcile the mortal sin of taking a human life with the state's obligation to defend human life and seek justice through the necessary employment of force. The theory itself applied not only to act of determining if war was just (*Jus ad bellum*), but its conduct as well (*Jus in bello*). The British Catholic hierarchy defended their support of the war on both bases, noting that the violation of Belgian neutrality constituted just cause in the name of right for intervention, and that the various outrages committed by the German Army in Belgium and France were evidence of the moral need to wage war on behalf of civilization.[26]

Conscription tested British Catholics and Protestants alike. In the United Kingdom proper, Catholic activists Francis Meynell and Stanley Morison established The Guild of the Pope's Peace in January 1916, after the government introduced conscription. Following Benedict XV's example, the group called for an immediate cease fire and the negotiation of a peace treaty, with the Vatican serving as neutral arbitrator. The response from pro-war Catholics was swift and furious. Sermons and pastoral letters took on a newly belligerent tone, urging the Entente powers to utterly crush German opposition as a precondition for peace. Again, here Cardinal Bourne expressed his opposition to any *status quo ante bellum* peace initiative.[27] Nevertheless, Catholics across the British Empire were united in their opposition to the policy. In Canada, Quebecois Catholics inaugurated a campaign of stubborn resistance to conscription that adopted the

---

[26] E. Oldmeadow, *Francis Cardinal Bourne* II, 116, cited in Beck, *Benedict XV and World War I*, 38–39.

[27] Beck, *Benedict XV and World War I*, 41.

language of peace that Pope Benedict XV had so adeptly articulated. Irish Australian Catholics, including the Archbishop of Melbourne, Daniel Mannix, joined with trade unionists and other pacifist groups in opposing conscription there.

Ireland itself was another matter entirely. After the ban on Catholic recruitment in Ireland was lifted in the late eighteenth century, the army became by some reckonings "probably the most Catholic institution of the British state."[28] Despite their significance – Irish Catholics made up some 30 percent of the British army in 1868 – they were not received as wholeheartedly as their English, Welsh, or Scots comrades. From the mid nineteenth century until the start of the war, Irish nationalist Fenianism was considered a seditious creed, one that was regularly ascribed to allegedly sympathetic Catholic chaplains in uniform and local civilian priests as well. Units that were suspected of harboring Fenian sympathies were frequently dispatched to garrison duty in far flung imperial stations or subjected to disciplinary confinement in barracks.[29]

By the end of the war, some 210,000 Irishmen, Protestant and Catholic, enlisted in the British Army, of whom some 40,000 died.[30] Most prominent in recruitment campaigns were the Irish Catholic bishops, who gave their unwavering support to voluntary enlistment to combat German militarism and to act on the behalf of the millions of French and Belgian Catholic civilians who were under German occupation. After the opening of the July 1916 offensive at the Somme, however, the initial enthusiasm for the war had cooled considerably. Of course, another factor was the Easter 1916 uprising. Irish nationalists couched their appeals for independence in language and rhetoric calculated to unify the island's majority Catholics. One outcome of the Easter uprising was the lack of interest in enforcing the

---

[28] Michael Snape, *The Redcoat and Religion: The Forgotten History of the British Soldier from the Age of Marlborough to the Eve of the First World War* (Routledge, 2005), 160.

[29] *Ibid.*, 160–163.

[30] Department of the Taoiseach, "The 1916 Rising," November 19, 2018. www .gov.ie/en/publication/986eaf-the-1916-rising/#world-war-i Accessed July 24, 2019.

conscription clauses of the British Military Service Act of 1916. The closest the British Military Service Act of January 1916 came to being enforced in Ireland was during the crisis of April 1918, when the German Spring Offensive nearly broke through the British Army's defenses. Rejected by both the Loyalist political establishment and Sinn Féin, the attempt to introduce Irish conscription was met with stiff resistance from the Irish bishops, who united to issue a declaration and pledge to resist a draft through all possible means. Their support for the demonstrations proved critical, and demonstrated the clear alignment of the Catholic Church with Irish Republicanism that followed.

The United States

When the United States entered the war, over fifteen million Americans claimed Catholicism as their primary faith, approximately 17 percent of the nation's population. At this time America was not only a majority Protestant nation, it also identified religion in purely subjective terms, with moral and racist overtones. Catholicism was viewed with open hostility and fear by many of the nation's Protestant majority, whose cultural and political worldviews were defined by white supremacy. Accordingly Protestant immigrants from northern and western European countries were normalized more rapidly than other Catholic, Eastern Orthodox, or Jewish arrivals. Each of these groups was seen as a potential threat to the stability of the status quo that benefited America's established white Anglo-Saxon Protestant population. Their alien professions of faith, along with their radical political philosophies and inferior racial stock, threatened to overwhelm the native-born majority.[31]

Like many Protestant denominations, American Catholics were outspoken in their objections to the war before April 1917. Pope Benedict XV's rejection of the war found a ready audience in the United States, where President Wilson's policy of neutrality was generally welcomed. This did

---

[31] Gordon L. Heath, ed., *American Churches and the First World War* (Pickwick Publications, 2016), 33; Kelly J. Baker, *Gospel According to the Klan: The KKK's Appeal to Protestant America, 1915–1930* (The University Press of Kansas, 2011), 44–45, 169–172.

not preclude open support by various immigrant communities for their own home country. German Catholics viewed the course of the war with great interest, celebrating the German Army's successes; French and Polish Catholics did the same with regard to the Entente powers. Irish Catholics were pro-German insofar as they were at war against the much-hated English. Proponents for American entry into the war viewed such partisanship as evidence of the questionable loyalty of the so-called "hyphenate Americans." German Americans in particular were accused of dual loyalties, giving rise to a wave of hatred and prejudice that would last through the war, even as younger men were volunteering and being conscripted into service.[32]

Nativist groups, while often focusing on the question of whether Catholics could demonstrate primary loyalty to the American Republic and the Constitution, also pursued a gendered critique that shared a language of racial exceptionalism. Catholic women were portrayed as weak, easily manipulated, and cowed into submission under threat of physical or sexual violence at the hands of their clergy. Children were painted as uncontrollable thugs-in-waiting, disdainful of authority and eager to embrace violence. Anti-Catholic groups like the American Protective Association spread scurrilous rumors throughout the country accusing Catholic priests and nuns of white slavery and child abuse in their schools and orphanages. As the United States watched the war in Europe from the sidelines, new accusations flew, portraying Pope Benedict XV as the Kaiser's stooge. American Catholics were portrayed as an internal danger, a fifth column preparing to launch an armed coup against Washington at Germany's instigation.[33]

Once fully engaged in the war, however, the most virulent anti-Catholic rhetoric abated. Attacks on American Catholics only served the interest of the German enemy, and had the potential to undercut national economic, industrial, and military mobilization. New hazards like Bolshevism also

---

[32] Heath, *American Churches and the First World War*, 34–35.

[33] Justin Nordstrom, *Danger on the Doorstep: Anti-Catholicism and American Print Culture in the Progressive Era* (University of Notre Dame Press, 2006), 6–7, 111–112, 128.

shifted nativist discourse away from a predominant anti-Catholic focus to a more nuanced – if no less racialized – target. The Church's fervent anti-socialism, particularly expressed in the dialogues accompanying the 1917 Fátima visions, helped direct attention away from existing prejudices. Philanthropic lay organizations like the Knights of Columbus further solidified the anti-Communist, pro-American credentials of Catholicism during the war.[34] Immigrant Catholics were accorded an almost honorary status as peer citizens by many prewar Protestant skeptics. American bishops may have had this outcome in mind when they rejected Pope Benedict XV's renewed calls for peace and arbitration in August 1917.[35] By following the direction of the state over their own moral and spiritual leader, American Catholics adopted the same nationalistic identity and loyalty motivating other national Church leaders in Europe.

Ultimately there should be no mistaking the motivation that drove the American Catholic community to embrace the war. As historian Justin Nordstrom observes, "Catholics, for their part, envisioned the Great War as an opportunity to demonstrate their profound national loyalties, enlisting for military duty in the thousands and participating in wartime service in greater proportions than their Protestant counterparts."[36] Anti-Catholicism remained part of the American nativist discourse after the First World War. The 1915 revival and subsequent popularity of the second Ku Klux Klan reveals the extent to which rural Protestants continued to distrust immigrant communities that were not Protestant. However, even as the new Klan represented a particularly virulent strain of nativism within the white Protestant community, its appeal was more directly tied to the declining social influence of traditional small-town and rural elites in the face of postwar modernity. Even as the Ku Klux Klan was claiming – and displaying – tremendous levels of support in middle America, its influence and power were crumbling in the face of a moral backlash by individuals and communities disgusted with the Klan's violent populism. The example of American Catholic support and participation in the war effort played

---

[34] Patrick Carey, "The First World War and Catholics in the United States," in Heath, *American Churches and the First World War*, 32–52, 45.

[35] *Ibid.*, 39–40.

[36] Nordstrom, *Danger on the Doorstep*, 193.

no small part in the effort to disabuse and resist the Klan in the decade after the war's end.[37]

The First World War and Protestantism

At the onset of the First World War, Protestantism was in a general state of flux. Recent schisms in belief and practice had provoked a general division between mainstream established traditions and newer nonconformist and evangelical churches. New biblical criticism challenged literal interpretations of scripture in every way, while the perception that secularist ideas like socialism and Darwinism were filtering into church doctrine was viewed by traditionalists as a dire challenge to their faith. Church attendance was slipping, particularly in urban and industrialized areas. In Great Britain and Germany the challenges were related to class and geography. In the United States, these same issues were joined by demographic shifts in the wake of decades of immigration. In all three nations, younger generations were moving away from traditional observations of faith to embrace a more politically and socially activist creed. The Social Gospel movement of the early twentieth century was intended at the start to promote equality through action and legislation. Where the new movement had sought to invigorate Protestantism in response to the challenges of industrialization and immigration, however, it actually provoked greater division within the established denominations.[38]

Another dimension of Western Protestantism that proved influential in the coming conflict was the appeal among upper- and middle-class youths of muscular Christianity. Rooted in a perceived crisis of masculinity gripping Western society, proponents of muscular Christianity believed mainstream Protestant doctrines were losing their appeal because of their emphasis on kindness, charity, and forbearance – all feminizing qualities. In the same moment, young men (and to a far lesser extent, young women) experienced greater anxiety, tension, and ultimately physical and moral degeneration in the wake of modern industrialization. The spiritual challenge was presented

---

[37] *Ibid.*, 202–206.

[38] Richard Schweitzer, *The Cross and the Trenches: Religious Faith and Doubt among British and American Great War Soldiers* (Praeger Publishers, 2003), 3–5.

as either continuing to permit the gradual "sissification" of boys through their exposure to inadequate expressions of faith, or to transform their bodies and souls into robust, athletic men in a holistic pursuit of sport, physical labor and competition, and hard work. The muscular Christianity movement emphasized conflict as a positive experience, as it tested the body and the soul together, a process that would be tested to the fullest in the trenches.

Traditionalist anxiety over a perceived decline of faith in Western Europe and the United States met headlong with a sense that the modernist critique of scripture and church history was undermining belief. Many took solace in Fundamentalism, an antimodernist evangelical movement that celebrated the literal interpretation of scripture with particular emphasis on the prophetic texts in the Bible. Appearing first in the United States, Fundamentalism was closely associated with the Pentecostal revival that followed the 1906 San Francisco earthquake. Both movements emphasized the end times prophecies in the Old and New Testaments and celebrated the appearance of miracles, including speaking in tongues and faith healing, as evidence of the divine made manifest in their church. Fundamentalist churches began to appear in all major denominations, particularly in the so-called Bible Belt – the southern, lower midwestern, and southwestern United States – as well as in rural Canada, Australia, Great Britain, and Germany.[39]

This collection of smaller anxieties and internalized conflicts within Protestantism became manifest as a cross-denominational acclaim for war. This was no mere nationalistic appeal for victory, though this did appear to be the case in much of the churches and state propaganda efforts. Eschatology, or end times theology, rather than material identification with the nation, informed this popular support for the war. From the 1890s forward, the purported need for a European war was touted through-out European intellectual circles – not to redefine political boundaries, or to resolve lingering passions for vengeance, but as a necessary tragedy to pave the way for religious renewal. Proponents considered that the next war

---

[39] Philip Jenkins, *The Great and Holy War: How World War I Became a Religious Crusade* (HarperCollins, 2014), 139–141.

would be short but brutal, but it would also create the seedbed for the growth of vibrant and new trans-European society, one sustained by a new appreciation for spiritual guidance.[40] Individually surprised when war broke out in August 1914, British and German clergymen quickly gathered their wits and championed the justice of their particular cause, calling down the spiritual weight of their faith against the enemy. Likewise, after the United States joined the war in April 1917, influential ministers and writers like Harry Emerson Fosdick saw the war as both crisis and opportunity. The crisis was obvious; the devastation and human cost of the war was expected to be high. The opportunity, though, was more nuanced. The anxieties and fears that would attend America's participation would give way to a religious revival as a trans-Atlantic reassessment of the need for faith and the Protestant church.[41]

Great Britain

Since the mid-1930s, many British military historians have considered how the war fractured the antebellum consensus that valued tradition and faith in daily life. According to Basil Henry Liddell-Hart, and later Leon Wolff and Alan Clarke, the war was a violent break with many traditional covenants made within British society, especially with regard to religion and faith.[42] But many trends, including secularization, had begun years before the war. Religious historian Michael Snape describes how prewar British society, while still acknowledging the role of faith and deliberate religious observance among the urban and rural working class, experienced a transition in belief reflecting the spread of secular values in daily life. "In the later decades of the nineteenth century," Snape writes, "the faith of the English middle and upper classes had been shaken as old religious certainties retreated in the face of biblical criticism, the advance of modern science

---

[40] Karen Armstrong, *Fields of Blood: Religion and the History of Violence* (Anchor Books, 2014), 298.

[41] Schweitzer, *The Cross and the Trenches*, 10–11.

[42] See Basil Henry Liddell-Hart, *The Real War, 1914–1918* (Little, Brown & Company, 1930, 1964); Leon Wolff, *In Flanders Fields, Passchendaele, 1917* (Penguin, 1959, 2001); Alan Clarke, *The Donkeys* (Pimlico, 1961).

and of a moral rebellion against the doctrine of eternal punishment."[43] Alan Wilkinson elaborates further, noting how the Anglican Church responded to modernization in its theology. While the Church tolerated intellectual critique of scripture and its own place in society, elders lamented how it was growing distant from the majority of Britons. Here the Church of England was increasingly seen as cut-off from the everyday needs and problems working-class families faced.[44] There were exceptions. Rural England and the Scottish Highlands retained a strong sense of religious devotion. High regard for tradition bolstered socially conservative views on religion in these rural areas, but social class hierarchies and deference cannot be discounted. In rural counties, the local gentry and landed aristocracy exerted tremendous influence on their tenants and workers. Analyses of Anglican participation and attendance point toward the means by which the rural churches were perceived as an agent of control by the social elite. Dominated by upper- and middle-class clergy with little to no cognitive tie to their farm worker flock, many felt that the church existed primarily to keep them in line.[45] Mission work in urban slums also appears to have fostered church attendance among those who faced bleak outlooks for survival. But overall, Snape notes, even among the working class, religious sentiment was waning in Protestant communities as the churches exercised less public outreach through charity and education. On the eve of the war, British religious temperament was wearing thin.

Britain's other mainstream Protestant denominations also supported the war. Clergymen used the pulpit to explain the moral imperatives at play in the trenches, providing congregations a measure of reassurance in the face of growing casualty lists and ambiguous press reporting. The churches accepted their role as interlocuter between the wartime state and its population with near total unanimity. Even the Quakers and other radical non-conformists, while retaining their pacifist outlook, refrained from outright criticism of the war. Other denominations, particularly the Anglican and

[43] Snape, *The Redcoat and Religion*, 3.

[44] Alan Wilkinson, *The Church of England and the First World War*. Third Edition (The Luttterworth Press, 2014), 5–6.

[45] Schweitzer, *The Cross and the Trenches*, 5.

Presbyterian majorities, took an even more active role in conveying Britain's moral imperative against a barbaric – if not unholy – foe. Ministers invoked a vigorous militancy in sermons and personal ministrations, presenting the war with Germany as a moral crusade that necessitated complete support and participation by their congregations. By aligning themselves with the state, the Protestant churches entrenched their legitimacy through their patriotic displays, further enshrining their place as part of the social hierarchy in British life.[46]

After the August 23, 1914 engagement at Mons and the subsequent British retreat, mobilization was not seen as a mere political calculation, it was portrayed as a just response to German militarism and cruelty. The unwarranted invasion of Belgium, with the accompanying brutality levied against its population, served as a warning to Britons of what was at stake in the war.[47] From the onset, just war discourse informed Britain's participation. Having no recourse, the British people were compelled to take a stand to defend Belgian sovereignty in the face of unwarranted aggression. It was a short step, however, from just war causality to embracing the violent discourse of holy war. As news of alleged and real atrocities was spread by the British government, ministers framed the conflict as a crusade against immoral German militarism and savagery. Historian Richard Schweitzer places this moment in 1915, sometime between Second Ypres and the fall Artois-Loos offensive. At this point, the last vestiges of hope for a short war evaporated as news of the British Expeditionary Force's near destruction sank in. Rhetorically the Germans changed from merely being "the enemy" into diabolical agents of Satan. Rumors of mass rape and mutilations, crucified Canadian soldiers, and corpse-rendering factories only fueled the holy war rhetoric. Belgium and France were but the first victims of German aggression that, unchecked, would spread across the English Channel and overwhelm decency and Christian civilization itself.[48]

---

[46] See Michael Snape and Edward Madigan, eds., *The Clergy in Khaki: New Perspectives on British Army Chaplaincy in the First World War* (Routledge, 2013).

[47] Stuart Bell, *Faith in Conflict: The Impact of the Great War on the Faith of the People of Britain* (Helion & Company, Limited, 2017), 39.

[48] Schweitzer, *The Cross and the Trenches*, 6–8.

As the war evolved from the open state of maneuver into trench stalemate, different perspectives on Anglican theology took shape. Writing in November 1916, Chaplain Neville Stuart Talbot argued that while organized observance and religious sentiment declined among British soldiers during the war, religiosity and Christian sentiment remained ever present in the trenches. Talbot considered the war in this regard a positive transformative experience. Anglicanism – if not all of Protestantism in England – had lost influence in the face of the totality of the war's violent reality in large part because of its dogmatic insistence upon the literal meaning of the Bible. What was once accepted with little question was being pried loose in the face of certain doom.[49] And yet Talbot, and others, saw this as a positive development that would ultimately reinforce the faith. By stripping away artifice and antiquated and erroneous tradition, the war was leaving behind a purer, more humane state of Christian belief. Prewar Christianity had become too distant from its flock, content with rote recitation and bland ritual. Such observance was completely alien to the immediate vibrancy of life in constant mortal danger men experienced in the trenches. The war was thus a necessary challenge to the state of the organized Anglican religion.[50]

Germany

German citizens greeted the war with a mixture of ecstatic support and muted skepticism. This was hardly unique – despite the image presented by photographs of crowds clamoring for war in every city, many Europeans were concerned about the prospect and cost of war. But as the immediate moment of mobilization orders and final diplomatic exchanges between the combatants passed, Germans did rally around familiar paternalist institutions for solace and moral support. Protestant and Catholic churches alike reported being full to capacity, as many people turned to religion for meaning. The moment was captured by Kaiser Wilhelm II in his famous August 4, 1914 appeal to German solidarity across class and religious lines.

---

[49] Neville Stuart Talbot, *Thoughts on Religion and the Front (Annotated)* (Macmillan and Company, 1917), 9.

[50] *Ibid.*, 15–17.

As *Reichstag* socialists lined up alongside conservative and liberal parties to cast near unanimous votes in favor of an emergency appropriation of five billion marks for the war, the Kaiser addressed the nation, exclaiming, "I no longer recognize any political parties, all I see are Germans!"[51] The spirit of the speech certainly applied to the political divisions in Germany, but it should also be taken as a direct acknowledgment of Wilhelm II's belief that the war united all Germans, irrespective of faith and creed.

The ecumenical character of the *Burgfrieden* speech has long defined the moment, and subsequent histories have painted it as a moment of civic pride and self-sacrifice in which all participants laid aside their regional and religious identities to become part of a larger, truly *völkisch* ideal. Other observers, however, have noted the Pentecostal character of the *Burgfrieden* idea. Borrowing from the English-speaking world's own movement, German Lutheran preachers saw direct divine inspiration in the war message of unity issued by the Kaiser and the German bishops. The politically and socially divided German Empire was transformed by war from a petty, secularized throng into a people sanctioned by God. Logically Germany should have been defeated easily by the larger armies and fleets of the Entente powers. Victories in the East and West, however, spoke toward something intangible, some type of divine inspiration behind their own successes. As a people engaged in a war for survival, Germans became a collective vessel for God's favor, as embodied in the Holy Spirit, which became the essential *Volksgeist* of the nation.[52]

This spirit of collective idealism and divine favor spread to inspire the intellectual and creative elites that stood apart from the masses. Academics, philosophers, and other intellectuals long complained that Germans were bewitched by the materialism of the modern era, giving up their spiritual independence to the superficial external pleasures of the marketplace and music hall. Making their own case for the justness of Germany's participation in the war, and the flawed purpose the Entente nations invoked to stand

---

[51] Quoted in Holger Afferbach, "Wilhelm II as Supreme Warlord in the First World War," *War in History*. 5:4 (November, 1998), 427–450, here 433.

[52] A. J. Hoover, *God, Germany, and Britain in the Great War: A Study in Clerical Nationalism* (Praeger Publishers, 1989), 12.

against her, German intellectuals hoped to demonstrate their own patriotism and uncritical belief of their divine inspiration. In 1914, German Protestant theologians, many of them world renowned biblical scholars and anthropologists, signed two separate declarations of Germany's right to self-defense, casting the war as a contest to preserve civilization itself against Western materialism, French atheism, British capitalism, and Russian barbarism. Intended in part to deflect criticism of German actions in neutral countries – primarily the United States – the twin manifestos sought to reveal the justness of the German war effort through the signatories' exhibited participation. The fact that dozens of German professors, theologians, scientists, historians, authors, and other intellectuals supported the war as a moral and just cause was not nearly as successful as hoped. British commentators in particular were able to successfully recast the two statements as evidence of a collective psychosis taking root within Germany, for example. Yet although the world failed to accept the logic presented by intellectuals for the war, the documents do offer examples of the extent to which the *Burgfrieden* mentality had infiltrated all aspects of German society in the first years of the war, a totality made all the more impressive by the extent to which Protestant theologians participated in it.[53]

The course of the war for Germany was convoluted, even contradictory. Early successes during the first season of maneuver were followed by a long spell of attritive warfare. So long as German forces held Belgium and northern France, they could claim victory. But such announcements rang hollow as casualty counts grew and food supplies shrank. Protestant and Catholic ministers and priests together created a volatile war theology – *Kriegstheologie* – to bolster public spirit as the spell of the *Burgfrieden* faded when wartime successes stalled. Sermons and lay messages took on both a more harsh and warlike tone and cast the war as an existential contest of the spirit. Considering how eagerly Germans, even the Lutheran clergy, accepted militarism as a positive virtue in peacetime, the appropriation of war metaphors should not come as a surprise. But the strident attacks on England as an enemy of German civilization now conspired with a new sense that darker forces were attempting to deny Germany's destiny. "Perfidious Albion" was

---

[53] Jenkins, *Great and Holy War*, 79–81.

no simple propaganda device; the phrase captured the essence of British malevolence, hypocrisy, and greed. Pastors noted the long history of British aggression, and the ease with which she used others to bleed for her.[54]

Again, Britain was the most frequent target of Protestant *Kriegstheologie* sermons, but the other Entente partners were not spared. In all cases, however, the primary message remained: Germany had acted to preserve her culture and civilization from assault by a cabal of enemies led by Great Britain. The *Kaiserreich* stood alone against the odds, an image that evoked Martin Luther's "Mighty Fortress" (*Ein feste Burg*), the struggle a test of German culture and morality. Militarism was not a stain on German culture, it embodied virtue and honor. The German spirit, its *Volksgeist*, was militant, but also honorable, in the eyes of most Lutheran pastors and bishops. Her cause was just, her spirit true. Victory would come as a sign of God's favor and the German spirit to prevail.

The United States

For over two and a half years, Americans struggled with their conscience as they followed news of the war in Europe. An overwhelming number of American Protestants rejected the call from interventionists to join the fight, citing the lack of justification and their own Christian values – peace, charity, and love – as reasons for remaining neutral. But the course of the fighting and the image of a callous, heartless Germany seemingly making war against common decency itself was hard to resist. Even before President Woodrow Wilson delivered his war message to Congress on April 2, 1917, the steady drip of German outrages and actions, real and imagined, convinced many that war was coming. The perception that the American people were dragged unwillingly into the First World War is misplaced, certainly when it comes to the middle and upper class Protestants in the eastern United States. They may have been reluctant to go to war, but they accepted it as a necessary evil in the face of German hostility.

Who were these reluctant advocates for war? Religious historian Jonathan H. Ebel notes they comprised a blend of both socially progressive mainstream denominations and combative Pentecostals:

---

[54] Hoover, *God, Germany, and Britain*, 53.

> "The men and women who helped fight the Great War were
> products of a society whose cultural and religious landscape
> was shaped by a particular understanding of faith, citizen-
> ship, and manhood in which all three converged in the realm
> of strenuous action. Struggle, strain, and sacrifice demon-
> strated and enhanced physical and spiritual vigor, vitalized
> American culture, and gave life to the American nation."[55]

Accordingly American Protestantism, regardless of the specific denominational affiliation, conveyed physical and moral activity. Strenuous in its invocation and practice, the American Christian churches advocated a faith that made their adherents slow to anger, but capable to take up arms in a righteous cause.

Another factor is the militant rhetoric that resides in the heart of American Protestant discourse. American churches did express the evangelical mission in stark military-style language. The quest for salvation was regularly portrayed as a wartime experience, with Satan giving direct battle with God's agents for souls. Men and women engaged in evangelical witnessing were self-styled "soldiers of God" who were committed to mortal combat against the Great Adversary. In the event of real war, it was an easy transition for martial Protestants to turn their rhetoric against the Germans. Language once reserved for religious war became part of the intellectual arsenal to sustain morale and inspire sacrifice.[56]

Where Theodore Roosevelt is often held up as the exemplar of the American muscular Christianity model, his political nemesis President Woodrow Wilson is most often portrayed as a studious, cautious academic, who led the United States into war with the careful pace and tenor of a prosecuting attorney, and an attention to detail associated with a college professor. Often overlooked are Wilson's own religious sensibilities and the extent to which he brought his own evangelical outlook on duty, honor, and martial faith to the war. The premise that the First World War was a holy war, as authors like Philip Jenkins and Alan Wilkinson have discussed in

---

[55] Jonathan H. Ebel, *Faith in the Fight: Religion and the American Soldier in the Great War* (Princeton University Press, 2010), 2.

[56] *Ibid.*, 3.

their respective works, is largely built upon the abstract analysis of the intersection between ecumenical sermons and pastoral letters and the actions of the state. Direct associations of secular and religious policies and intentions are rare within the Western European fronts and their participants. Of course there are the "*Gott mit uns*" and the "God, King, and Country" sentiments all sides expressed, but these were largely casual appeals to the moral legitimacy of their cause. The United States under President Wilson is a different case study. Here the idea of the war as a moral crusade, one which would require the full cooperation and power of the state subordinated to the war effort, was made real.

Through his first term in office, Wilson constantly invoked America's righteous mission to bear witness of Christ to the world through deed and word. By aligning the United States and its foreign policy with an evangelical mission, President Wilson set the nation on a course toward war with Germany from the start of the conflict. As early as December 1915, Wilson began describing parallel connections between civic patriotism and Christian idealism in public addresses. To fulfill its destiny, the United States and its good Christian citizens would need to bolster itself for war, not for wealth, power, or other gain, but to make real the success of Christianity at large. The war was most certainly not a sign that faith and Christianity had failed. It was an epic test of faith and belief, one that Wilson and other proponents believed was set out to raise the United States above all other nations as the model of a godly state – the so-called "'Christ-nation' in world affairs."[57] For Christianity to advance to its premillenarian stage, it was necessary for the world to suffer a cataclysmic event – something like the Great War that was convulsing Europe. It was the United States' obligation to take part in this suffering, to experience a national Calvary, before taking its place among other countries as the most blessed and righteous of nations.[58]

For Woodrow Wilson and the progressive American Protestant clergy that supported him, the First World War was more akin to a crusade, not

---

[57] Richard M. Gamble, *The War for Righteousness: Progressive Christianity, The Great War, and the Rise of the Messianic Nation* (ISI Books, 2003), 133.

[58] *Ibid.*, 137.

only against the evils of German militarism, but one that would set America on the path to righteousness. The religious rhetoric employed to justify America's participation was not only broadly based, it reached down and resonated among average citizens to a degree not seen elsewhere.[59] Bold announcements of divine inspiration and the holy nature of the American cause to rescue humanity from the abyss were more than propagandist scrawling. Where Europe had become the site of mankind's Calvary, America was the avenging angel, delivering God's wrath upon the Kaiser and his minions. At the same time, Americans were admonished not to become so proud of their role as to ignore their own faults and flaws. The war was a golden opportunity to refresh American society, from sweeping the nation clean of vice and intemperance, to reaffirming the primacy of Protestantism as the bulwark of identity.[60]

Judaism and the War Experience

From Dublin to Kiev, European Jews were members of a loose-knit community often forced together in response to external prejudice. From the eighteenth century, prosperous Jewish communities acquired a more cosmopolitan outlook, seeking to become culturally more like their ennobled gentile neighbors. Outside of Russia and the eastern fringe of Austria-Hungary, Jews were assimilating into their individual national identities, becoming "less" Jewish and "more" European. Conservative and Reform schools of doctrine became more prevalent, as Western Jews left behind the self-imposed social seclusion that had been the rule since the Medieval era. The First World War was a great disruptor of the pan-European identity shared by the 80 percent of global Jews who resided there. In the end, the seeds for this community's future destruction were spread across Central Europe. But at the time, the war also provided tremendous opportunities for the prospective total integration of European Jews into their respective nations across most of Europe, even as

---

[59] Barry Hankins, *Woodrow Wilson: Ruling Elder, Spiritual President* (Oxford University Press, 2016), 157.

[60] Becker, *War and Faith*, 7, 108–109.

they would shudder from the compromises that were made with ferocious and notorious anti-Semitic actors.[61]

One commonly accepted "truth" of history is that European and American Jews were as a rule denied access to military service by their gentile secular societies. There were exceptions of course, but they serve as cautionary tales of the extent to which the state would go to break them. The 1894 incarceration of Captain Louis Dreyfus on false charges of espionage, and the ensuing political crisis that dominated *fin de siècle* France through 1906, is the most cited case. A much-heralded example of the biases within the French Army's officer corps against Jewish citizens, the Dreyfus case also reveals the depth of anti-Semitism within statist narratives of nationalism and militarism. Across Europe, military service was credited as the most explicit venue for expressing nationalist identity.[62] At the same time, however, this narrative was explicitly Christian oriented. Hyper-nationalists across Europe expressed citizenship in terms of acceptable religious profession. For them, Christian faiths – Catholicism, Eastern Orthodoxy, and mainstream Protestantism – were legitimized by their historic militancy. Centuries of religious war in Europe, though long considered *passé* in polite secular society, retained a hold on the public imagination even in the more liberally minded nations.[63] Great Britain, for example, constructed a large part of its national identity through the experience of the English Civil War (1642–1646) and the subsequent debate over Catholic legitimacy in a Protestant nation. Following unification, Germany remained in thrall to its cultural partition following the Thirty Years War, two hundred years before. The memories of these emphatically religious conflicts limited their realization in Europe proper, but they continued to resonate in the imperial sphere. The

---

[61] For details on Austria's Jewish community, see Marsha Rozenblit, *Reconstructing a National Identity: The Jews of Hapsburg Austria during World War I* (Oxford University Press, 2001).

[62] See George C. Mosse, *Fallen Soldiers: Reshaping the Memory of the World Wars* (Oxford University Press, 1990), 53–55; Eugen Weber, *Peasants into Frenchmen: The Modernization of Rural France, 1870–1914* (Stanford University Press, 1976), 298–302.

[63] Mosse, *Fallen Soldiers*, 35.

acquisition and exploitation of colonies in Africa and Asia was undertaken as a modern-day crusade by no small number of military officers and colonial administrators. Christianity was further entwined with cultural militarism to better define the state and its people on the eve of the First World War. Citizens were defined not only by their birthright, but by their willingness to sacrifice their own lives in the name of the nation. For Christians, this sacralization was a simple matter of course; if called upon of course they would follow the example of Christ for the larger community. Jews, unfortunately, were generally denied a chance to join in this larger communion, not only because of crude racial stereotypes and pseudo-scientific constructions, but because they remained alien to the larger Christian whole. Residing among and within Christian Europe, they were nevertheless considered interlopers even as they sought greater cultural assimilation. Denying Jews access to the rites of citizenship through military service on the basis that they were alien to the Christian idea of the nation exacerbated anti-Semitism across European society. Only with the mass conscription of the First World War were Jews accepted into Western military forces, and even here, only for the duration of the war. At best, their service would be soon forgotten. Or it would be transformed into something more sinister, as the rise of the *dolchstoss* legend in Germany shows.

The truth lay somewhere between the two extremes. Educated and socially conscious Jewish families sought and acquired some degree of integration into military institutions during the late nineteenth century. Access was generally limited to the technical branches where schooling in mathematics, engineering, and chemistry was held at a premium. In France and Great Britain, Jews entered the artillery and engineering branches in far greater proportion than the line branches. Both the infantry and cavalry remained the exclusive domain of established families of high or noble birth – and were Christian exclusively. There were greater opportunities in territorial and imperial forces, both being considered auxiliary military organizations with less prestige and greater expense. Even these were limited, however, to families with long ancestral lines in the two countries.[64]

[64] Derek J. Penslar, *Jews and the Military: A History* (Princeton University Press, 2013), 85–87.

Two of the most important outcomes of the war for Jews were related to Zionism and the transformation of anti-Semitism. Theodore Herzl's idea of a nationalistic Jewish state was originally framed around the secular Jewish community's backlash against the growing presence of Orthodox migrants from Eastern Europe in cosmopolitan Berlin, Vienna, and other Central European cities. Before the war, it was largely dismissed within the mainstream Jewish community as a fantasy. For a time, the German General Staff entertained the prospect of reaching an accommodation with Jews to craft a Jewish state in Eastern Europe. The idea of a Zionist homeland in the East was connected with early war efforts to create a protectorate for Russian Jews who were repeatedly targeted for pogroms. German Zionist leader Max Bodenheimer considered an autonomous region in Poland and the Ukraine, approximating the boundaries of the Russian Pale of Settlement and under German military protection, critical. Palestine, then still under Ottoman control, was too far for many European Jews and had a thoroughly insufficient infrastructure to accommodate a mass migration. Before the war, the United States was the favorite site for Jewish immigration; now the war and growing anti-immigrant sentiment ruled out further travel. Germany and Western Europe also didn't want to play host to millions of prospective migrants. A Jewish homeland in Eastern Europe, where the most Jews were, was far more practical to Bodenheimer, to other Zionists, and most importantly, to the army's inspector general, Erich Ludendorff. Zionist plans for an Eastern European homeland dovetailed perfectly with his own agenda for the occupied territories (*Ober Ost*). Unlike the region's other nationalities – Polish, Ukrainian, Lithuanian – the Eastern Jews were cooperative and openly supportive of their German occupiers, winning over Ludendorff's admiration and support. Ludendorff retained a large number of Jewish officers on the *Ober Ost* staff, where they administered the region and ameliorated the worst oppression targeting Jews. In 1917, however, as news of Woodrow Wilson's own calls for self-determination took hold, Ludendorff abandoned this earlier tolerance as he realized that the cooperation of other minorities – particularly Poles and other nationalities on the scene – was more politically viable. As he embraced these groups, he adopted the anti-Semitism that was all too prevalent there, ultimately becoming a leading figure in the far-right on the basis of this so-called political necessity.[65]

Just like the Christian faiths, Zionism split down the middle when it came to the question of support for the war. Some strived to recognize the transnational aspects of their religious and political identities and struggled with the dilemma of facing fellow Jews across No Man's Land. For most Zionists, the prospect of killing their brethren was less burdensome when balanced against the prospect of civic recognition in return for military service.[66] With the imminent and expected defeat of the Ottomans, British Zionists in particular considered a Jewish state in Palestine achievable. By mid-1917, Lord Rothschild and Chaim Weizman were able to successfully press their case for a postwar Zionist state in Palestine with the British war government and received a pre-negotiated declaration of British support for the future Israeli state in November. The Balfour Declaration had no direct power of mandate, but it did present the first state recognition of the Zionist ideal, setting the stage for the postwar British Mandate control of Palestine and other national acts of recognition, including by the United States.

Anti-Semitism remained pervasive throughout the war, even as Jews sought recognition and assimilation through their military service and civilian support for the war. Prior to the war, Imperial Russia pursued the most virulent anti-Semitic policies in Europe. Since 1791 Jews were restricted to living in the Pale of Settlement: Western Russia, Ukraine, Belarus, the Baltic states, Moldova, and Russian Poland. Even here, they remained subject to official harassment, local intolerance, and periodic violent pogroms. Accusations of disloyalty and usury were exacerbated after the 1903 release of the bogus *Protocols of the Elders of Zion*. The forgery attracted a widespread global audience, but it was primarily employed by Russian extremists to justify deeper anti-Semitic attacks and policies

---

[65] Tracey Hayes Norrell, *For the Honor of Our Fatherland: German Jews on the Eastern Front During the Great War* (Lexington Books, 2017), 10–11, 113–114; David J. Fine, *Jewish Integration in the German Army in the First World War* (DeGruyter, 2012), 71–94.

[66] Penslar, *Jews and the Military*, 144–145.

intended to further restrict Jewish access to public life.[67] The reality of Russian anti-Semitism was strong enough to frame a sort of moral quandary for Jews in the other Entente nations: specifically, how and why should English and French Jews take part in a conflict that aligned their wartime actions with such a ferocious regime? The only counter to this serious question was the hope that some measure of the tolerance and openness Western European Jews experienced might transfer to Russia through the course of the wartime alliance.

Jews in the United States

In the United States, Jews walked a very delicate line. For the most part recent arrivals to the country, they remained subject to stark racist and anti-Semitic prejudices. In some ways these anxieties were connected to existing class and ethnic divisions in American society. Nativist sentiments were high throughout the Progressive Era; America was not only a majority Protestant country, it was also deeply influenced and affected by a host of anti-Catholic and anti-Jewish ideas. Arriving primarily from Eastern Europe, by 1910 Jewish immigrants became the largest group of new arrivals to the United States. Settling primarily in northeastern cities, they became visible competitors with Italian and Irish immigrants for influence and resources. In New York City, for example, Jews made up a quarter of the city's population by 1917, with the majority residing in the small Lower East Side neighborhood of Manhattan island.[68] In many ways, Jews arriving from Russia and Austria-Hungary were model immigrants. Quick students of American culture and the English language, Eastern European Jews quickly assimilated into their new home's way of life. As the new Jewish Americans acquired stability, wealth, and local political heft, they continued to run up against prejudice, much informed by centuries-old anti-Semitic

---

[67] Theodore R. Weeks, "Jews and Others in Vilna-Wilno-Vilnius," in Omer Bartov and Eric D. Wentz, *Shatterzone of Empires: Coexistence and Violence in the German, Habsburg, Russian, and Ottoman Borderlands* (Indiana University Press, 2013), 87; Jenkins, *Great and Holy War*, 241–242.

[68] Richard Slotkin, *Lost Battalions: The Great War and the Crisis of American Nationality* (Owl Books, 2005), 87.

tropes and beliefs. Most of the anti-Semitic slurs were just that, verbal taunts and insults, calculated to remind the new arrivals of their alien status within a Protestant country. But Jewish immigrants also ran the risk of becoming victims of violence, especially in rural American settings. The 1915 lynching of Leo Frank, a Jewish factory manager who was identified as the assailant of Mary Phagan, a thirteen year old worker, in a flawed trial, was even at the time noted as being an extraordinary case of ethnically motivated violence.[69]

Jewish women in particular embraced the progressive cause, and sought to exercise some agency through social and political activism. Additionally, Jewish middle-class and working-class men and women alike were vehement in their opposition to the war. Some took this course as an extension of their own rejection of violence, born from their faith traditions and inculcated through living in places where resistance against slurs and insults was seen as an act of hostile defiance, often prompting a harsh wave of retaliatory pogroms by their Christian neighbors. Other observers credited a more overtly alien political ideology to Jews arriving in the United States. Imperial Russia had long been considered the most hostile and violently anti-Semitic country in the world. Millions of émigrés left in the preceding decades to escape the sting of prejudice and the violence of pogroms. Memories of Tsarist antipathy toward Jews lingered, and for many activists, served to block any sympathy for the Allied cause. After the March 1917 revolution toppled the Romanovs, their opposition lessened; but only after the subsequent November 1917 revolution did the majority of activists openly support the war effort – reasoning that victory would not only eject the Germans from Russia, it would also topple the Bolsheviks as well.[70]

When the United States entered the war in April 1917, and subsequently inaugurated wartime conscription, Jewish Americans were immediately accused by nativists of shirking and draft dodging. Within the Regular Army, this view held sway among officers, many convinced

---

[69] See Steve Oney, *And the Dead Shall Rise: The Murder of Mary Phagen and the Lynching of Leo Frank* (Vintage, 2004).

[70] Penslar, *Jews and the Military*, 155.

Jews – especially recent migrants from Eastern Europe – were all more interested in money than honorable civic service.[71] According to the National Museum of American Jewish Military History, over 225,000 Jews served in the American military during the First World War. In every major urban Jewish community, draft boards reported strong compliance. Jewish social philanthropic groups organized into the Jewish Board for Welfare Work in the United States Army and Navy (later the Jewish Welfare Board) to offer material and inspirational support for Jewish military members. Considering the size of the new army, and the substantial presence of Jewish soldiers in several critical divisions, the Jewish Welfare Board's work was cut out for it. Some organizations, like New York's 77th Division, boasted large Jewish participation, with soldiers coming from neighborhoods and city blocks all over Manhattan and Brooklyn. The challenge for Jewish soldiers was both to receive adequate training to fight and survive in the field, and also to win respect and acceptance in the barracks and parade ground. A host of skills were employed to accomplish this task, many legitimate exercises of skill and street smarts. If necessary, there was no shortage of tough urban Jews willing to defend their faith and their identity with their fists as well.[72]

For all of their heroism and accomplishments in France, Jewish soldiers continued to face constant slurs and insults. Compared with other nationalities and ethnicities, the Jewish soldiers in the 77th Division were considered more of a "problem" by officers (almost all of them Anglo-Saxon Protestants) than a boon for decades after the war. Charges of malingering, shirking, desertion, and cowardice dogged Jewish soldiers in public accounts of the A.E.F.'s Meuse-Argonne campaign. Other accusations of political unreliability, particularly claims that Jewish soldiers were more vulnerable to Bolshevik recruiting efforts, were calculated to buttress prewar claims of their inability to assimilate with mainstream American Protestant culture. Then there were the Social Darwinists and eugenicists, all of whom rejected the prospect of assimilation altogether, fearful that

---

[71] Joseph W. Bendersky, *The "Jewish Threat": Anti-Semitic Politics of the U.S. Army* (Basic Books, 2000), 38.

[72] Slotkin, *Lost Battalions*, 104–108.

interbreeding with white Americans would only accelerate the slow degeneration of the race. Such accusations and charges, no matter how scurrilous and false in fact, appeared in the memoirs of veteran officers through the 1970s, revealing how deeply anti-Semitism had permeated mainstream society, and how fleeting and uncaring these men were toward those who served under their direction.[73]

Turning back to the efforts to combat anti-Semitism, the field work of the Jewish Welfare Board was significant not only for the immediate needs of soldiers; it also went far toward easing the assimilation of the Jewish community in the United States. Of course anti-Semitism remained a significant challenge – indeed, in the ensuing decade, hostility toward Jews increased in many parts of the United States. But through constant interaction with other Protestant and Catholic chaplains, and the sharing of scarce resources to fulfill the overall role of ministering to the spiritual needs of the millions of soldiers and sailors in camps, on ships, and in the trenches, the civilians in the Jewish Welfare Board and the fifty-five uniformed military rabbis charted a new, more inclusive dialogue between native-born Anglo/Irish Americans and the largely Eastern European Jewish immigrant community.[74]

Ultimately American Jews viewed their community's participation in the First World War with a fair degree of ambiguity. Going into the war, Jews saw an opportunity to receive cultural legitimacy and acceptance by the majority white Protestant society. To a degree, they were successful. Jews and Catholics alike were touted by reporters and future chroniclers in print and film of the war as essential components of a larger, diverse American comity, partners in a Judeo-Christian heritage who were further united by their participation in a largely secularized institution where religious privilege was laid aside. And yet, where members of the community had once sought full assimilation as an ideal solution, following Theodore Roosevelt's admonition against "hyphenated-Americans," returning veterans also came to further value the unique qualities of their faith that distinguished them from other Americans. As historian Jessica

---

[73] *Ibid.*, 498–500; Bendersky, *The "Jewish Threat,"* 39, 41–43.

[74] Slomovitz, *Fighting Rabbis* 44–50.

Cooperman notes, "They may have been happy to see the fences between men disappear, but they had no desire to see Judaism itself disappear. For many, the preservation of Judaism required the protection of Jewish homes."[75] Assimilation was all good and well, but not at the expense of the individual and collective Jewishness of the soldier and their community.

Jews in the German Army

Given the appeal of the so-called *Sonderweg* question – that is, the existence of a "special" anti-Semitic path in German culture that essentially doomed its Jewish population – studies into the extent of Jewish integration into wartime society are not surprising.[76] This scholarship offers valuable insights into both the cosmopolitan nature of Wilhelmine society and the extent to which casual anti-Semitism was accepted as a given. On the one hand, Germany was considered "the best European nation for Jews," the two peoples the most like-minded in temperament and outlook.[77] Emancipated during the Napoleonic era, Jews were given full rights as citizens after 1871. German Jews took great pride in their civic identity and sought assimilation as well as they achieved prosperity. Anti-Semitism persisted, but as its appeal declined among more cosmopolitan elites, it became a device that nationalists and rightists trotted out during times of political or national crisis. The high mark was in 1891, when the imperialist Pan-German League was founded and adopted harsh rhetoric against German Jews. This tone soon shifted as cultural hostility faded. Many Germans looked at the ongoing pogroms and persecution taking place in Russia as proof of the dehumanizing and unsettling path anti-Semitism laid out.

---

[75] Jessica Cooperman, *Making Judaism Safe for America: World War I and the Origins of Religious Pluralism* (New York University Press, 2018), 146.

[76] Daniel Jonah Goldhagen's *Hitler's Willing Executioners: Ordinary Germans and the Holocaust* (Vintage, 1997). See also Geoff Eley, *The "Goldhagen Effect": History, Memory, Nazism—Facing the German Past*. Social History, Popular Culture, and Politics in Germany (University of Michigan Press, 2000).

[77] Norrell, *For the Honor of Our Fatherland*, xiv, quote on xvi.

Before unification, the military was – save for a flurry of field commissions during the Franco-Prussian War – virtually free of Jewish officers. This would continue through the years before the First World War. A few wealthy young Jewish men would receive commissions following the personal intervention of the Kaiser – and even here, such action was often forthcoming only after promises of conversion to Christianity were made. Otherwise the level of commissioning varied from state to state within the German Empire. Bavaria, considered one of the more liberal kingdoms in Germany, commissioned fifty Jewish reserve lieutenants in 1907. In Prussia, only a handful of young Jewish men were granted the reserve commission before 1885, and none after until the war began. The obstacle here was purely prejudicial. In the Prussian state military, commission seekers needed the full assent of the regiment's officers. Jewish applicants were regularly blackballed for unspecified reasons.[78]

Ultimately military expediency and the toll of battle changed the Army's attitude toward Jewish officers. Long denied commissions in the Prussian army, and only recently allowed access to the officer corps in Bavaria, Jews were excluded on a complex rationale that equated their religious identity with their perceived gender characteristics. Accordingly, Jews did not possess the characteristics that would qualify them for military service as a "martial race." Indeed, in Germany they were seen as being the exact opposite: an innately craven and unheroic people, thoroughly unsuited for military service, and certainly not for commissioning as officers. Some Jews rejected this labeling, and pursued commission through alternative paths, including as reserve officers, via conversion to Christianity, or through enlistment in more Jewish-friendly German states like Bavaria where they could obtain a commission. The war soon changed this. In August 1914, Kaiser Wilhelm II opened the way, ordering the Prussian army to accept Jewish cadets into reservist officer training. Considering that reservists were already being called up for regular service, the Kaiser's edict effectively cleared the hurdles restricting Jewish commissioning. By the end of the war, two thousand Jews served as officers. None achieved a grade higher than that of Captain (*Hauptmann*), but their appearance was taken as

---

[78] Penslar, *Jews and the Military*, 89.

a signal that Germany was becoming more open and accepting of its Jewish citizens.[79]

German Jews continued to face anti-Semitic prejudice and attacks. As the war dragged on, both Protestant and Catholic communities turned their frustration toward the Jewish community. Nationalistic and anti-Semitic conservatives were particularly skeptical of claims of Jewish solidarity and participation in the larger war effort, driven by a sense of impotence as the stalemate on all fronts dragged on. Jews were not the only minority targeted by vigilant Germans; the loyalty of Poles, French speakers from Alsace and Lorraine, and sectarian Christian groups was also considered suspect. This was in keeping with the spirit of the *Burgfrieden* championed by the Kaiser from the war's inception. Taking a page from Lutheran theology, pro-war nationalists styled Germany as a "mighty fortress" (*"feste Burg"*), under assault from without and within. By steeping the call to arms in Protestant rhetoric, other religious communities – Catholic and Jewish – were cast as historic threats to the German wartime effort. Food shortages resulting from poor management and the British naval blockade added to the general distrust of the Jewish community by other Germans. Baseless rumors of Jews hoarding food, or of department stores owned by Jews gouging their gentile customers, spread across the country. Attempts to equate the sacrifices made by Jewish families with their Protestant and Catholic neighbors ensued.[80] In response, journals and magazines were dedicated to recounting the biographies of Jewish soldiers, living and deceased, to emphasize the normalcy of the community in comparison with their gentile neighbors. In 1916, inspired by the drumbeat of anti-Semitic accusations, the military compiled a census of Jewish soldiers and officers. This *Judenzählüng* ("Jew count") served mixed purposes. On the one hand, it offered direct evidence that Germany's Jewish population was fully behind the war effort. Over 100,000 Jews were revealed to have entered the military. These were not rear-echelon soldiers – seven out of every ten men served in combat units, predominantly infantry, on all fronts. By the

---

[79] Tim Grady, *A Deadly Legacy: German Jews and the Great War* (Yale University Press, 2017), 7–8, 70.

[80] Grady, *A Deadly Legacy*, 119–124.

end of the war, over 12,000 German Jews were killed in action. Some 7,000 would receive field commissions as officers, while another 35,000 were decorated for courage under fire. In all, approximately 17 percent of all German Jews served in the army during the war, roughly equal to that of all other citizens.[81]

Nevertheless the census revealed the full extent to which anti-Semitic bias had infiltrated wartime German society. The census was not ordered to protect the reputation of the German Jewish community, but to prove the validity of the scurrilous claims against them. When the results were compiled, and gave clear evidence that Jews were suffering alongside their fellow Germans, and not profiting from their misery, the report was suppressed. This was not just a matter of cognitive dissonance on the part of the German high command. The report not only contradicted deeply held biases and presumptions about the Jewish community, it also challenged the idea that the Second Reich was first and foremost a Christian state. As long as Jews remained outsiders, existing within the empire as a distinct minority group dependent upon the tacit grace of the rest of the state, the primacy of German identity as a Christian people remained intact. The results of the *Judenzählüng* turned these assumptions upside down. Solid Jewish support and participation in the war effort undercut the racial and religious exceptionalism validating and defining German identity.[82]

Alternatively Jews were outraged that their civic commitment to the war, and Germany itself, was considered suspect. Little could be done about the informal and casual anti-Semitism that flourished among their neighbors; here they could only offer the example of lives of sacrifice and civic and private mourning for the dead. Before the 1916 census, secular and religious Jews alike felt that they were becoming more accepted across German society. Plans were even being considered to take advantage of the German military's successes in the East to expand public outreach to rural Jews in occupied Poland and Byelorussia. At the time, the census was denounced by many in the Jewish community as another example of overt anti-Semitism. Many prominent Jewish intellectuals allegedly reconsidered

[81] Norrell, *For the Honor of Our Fatherland*, 88.
[82] Grady, *A Deadly Legacy*, 137–142.

their support for the war and began to doubt if there was a place for Jews in postwar Germany. However some note the census was – at first – more inconvenience than outrage. Historian Derek Penslar notes mention of the census was infrequent among civilian letters to the front. He further notes it was more frequently mentioned in the press after 1933, giving impetus to both the notion that the intention of the census was to validate existing anti-Semitic attitudes and that within the Jewish community, the entire project was considered important only in how it reflected upon their wartime activities and patriotism.[83]

Russian Orthodoxy and the War

One of the most famous photographs of the arrival of war in 1914 is of Tsar Nicholas II on horseback, offering a blessing to a company of soldiers, all of whom are kneeling before their absolute monarch and the religious icon he holds before them. Few photos capture the essence of the Russian Orthodox relationship with the monarchy and the peasantry. Orthodoxy was the state religion, but its status was in many ways more secure than that of other faiths in other countries. The Church was very much the interlocutor translating imperial edicts for the masses; likewise the monarchy relied heavily upon the Orthodox establishment for details about the people. Nevertheless, the war transformed the relationships between Church and people as well as the relationships of both with the state. The Orthodox Church, in its role as the official state church, was expected not only to offer total support to the state, but also to serve as the direct channel to the rural peasantry for the regime. Clergy were expected to make regular reports on the successful prosecution of the war, and to use their position to make appeals for subscriptions to war loans. They were also put in the position of reporting to the government, through their normal hierarchical channels to the upper levels of the Synod, on the mood of the peasants as the war progressed. Overall the record of the clergy was mixed. Many priests were dismissed by their flocks as meddling lackeys, eager to supplement their meager wages and lackluster status at the expense of their congregations.

[83] Penslar, *Jews and the Military*, 173, 178–179; Fine, *Jewish Integration in the German Army*, 14–16.

Wartime attendance actually dropped during the war, as many civilians were called to wartime labor service schemes, which pulled them away from the Church. There was also the news of mismanagement and incompetence within the Church. A regular feature of back-pew gossip in peacetime, the tabloid-style rumors of monks and clergymen like Grigori Rasputin – men who exploited gullible faithful congregants for their own licentious desires and petty influence – fueled skepticism as to the Church's real interests and agenda.[84]

At the start of the war, Russians accepted the idea that the war against Germany was a holy war. As David Stone notes, this was not an easy prospect. The alliances with Catholic France and Protestant England imbued the war with an ecumenical cast that did not align well with the idea of an Orthodox crusade against Lutheran and Catholic Germany and Austria-Hungary. Stone notes it took a careful negotiation of identities to create a perspective that the real enemy was German militarism, not its Protestant faith. Thus "the war was one of liberation, but liberation of whom and from what was not particularly clear."[85]

Unfortunately many soldiers considered violence against Jews to be part of this liberation struggle. The 1914 campaigns in Galicia and Russian Poland were accompanied by a drumbeat of atrocities against Jewish communities and families. The anti-Semitic violence was no surprise to German and Austrian Jews, who responded with greater support and loyalty to the Central Powers' war effort. Throughout the region, Polish civilians joined in the massacres, either directing Russian soldiers to hiding places or taking action themselves. Pogroms became a tool of military expediency, proponents arguing their actions were justified as they removed a hostile enemy population.[86]

The theaters where the Russian Army was engaged were distinctly different from the Western Front, not only in topography and engineering,

---

[84] Peter Gatrell, *Russia's First World War: A Social and Economic History* (Pearson Longman, 2005), 76–77, 102.

[85] David R. Stone, *The Russian Army in the Great War: The Eastern Front, 1914–1917* (University Press of Kansas, 2015), 211.

[86] Norrell, *For the Honor of Our Fatherland*, 6–13; Jenkins, *Great and Holy War*, 261.

but also in the transfer and exchange of cultural identities. Orthodox soldiers – notably Cossack cavalry forces – expressed their religious chauvinism in regular massacres of Jewish, Catholic, and Muslim communities in these frontline areas. Explained away as random acts of violence committed by an overeager group of zealous soldiers, said accounts fail to consider how Orthodox chaplains and junior officers goaded their men to action upon arriving in these alien communities.[87] Most critically, these atrocities were not isolated incidents or random expressions of intolerance. Historian Peter Holquist notes that ethnic and religious violence followed a clear path of legitimization, being "derived from 'standard operating procedure' – an operating procedure that was utilitarian and callous. The Russian military entirely subordinated the regions and their populations to its own military operations."[88] While Holquist here speaks directly toward Russian acts of ethnic cleansing in the Caucasus, he acknowledges similar actions taking place – under a far more ruthless and racist agenda – in Galicia targeting Jews. Accordingly the Russian Army engaged in extreme violence against religious and ethnic civilian minorities throughout its spheres of operation. Tellingly this violence was not associated with a formal expansionist policy, but rather reflected deeply seated cultural biases and prejudices that elevated Orthodox communities over other religious groups.[89]

The Church's reputation was not helped by its visibly mercurial attitude toward the Tsar and the government in 1917. At the onset of the war, the chief bishops were overt supporters of the war, appearing alongside Nicholas II in parades and in encampments bearing aloft the most holy icons of the Orthodox faith, bestowing their blessing upon the Tsar and his soldiers. Through 1917, the Church continued to offer unwavering public

---

[87] Alexander V. Prusin, "A 'Zone of Violence': The Anti-Jewish Pogroms in Eastern Galicia in 1914–1915 and 1941," in Bartov and Weitz, *Shatterzone of Empires*, 362–377, here 368–370.

[88] Peter Holquist, "Forms of Violence During the Russian Occupation of Ottoman Territory and in Northern Persia (Urmia and Astrabad), October 1914-December 1917," in Bartov and Weitz, *Shatterzone of Empires*, 334–361, here 338.

[89] *Ibid.*, 353.

support to the regime, no matter the outcome of the fighting in Poland and Ukraine. With the March Revolution, however, the Church immediately reversed its traditional opposition to representative government, joining parliamentarians to support the Tsar's abdication. Church officials claimed they were acting for the sake of Russia itself, to sustain a flagging war effort against her mortal enemies.[90] Perhaps, but for the growing masses of skeptical peasants and urban workers – not to mention the millions of war-weary soldiers – the Church's actions smacked of personal interest and profit. Long before the Bolsheviks portrayed the Orthodox Church as a parasitical institution, ordinary Russians had come to view the Church as opportunistic, more loyal to its own interests and desires than the needs of the people. The collapse of the Church-run orphanage system after 1917 only fed into this distrust. Thousands of orphaned children were turned out onto the streets, left to fend for themselves and becoming a visible sign of the immorality of the Church's hierarchy for its foes. The collapse of the regime in 1917 paved the way for the corrosion of public trust in the Orthodox Church, making it a ripe target for Bolshevik sanction in 1918 and after. The dismantling of the Church's property and power was not done in absence of public support. The Bolshevik government's legislative campaign against the Orthodox establishment succeeded because the people had lost faith in the Church long before January 1918, particularly in areas related to family and social welfare.[91]

The Ottoman Empire: Islam and the War

The Ottoman Empire entered the war on October 29, 1914, signaling its affiliation with Germany and Austria-Hungary by shelling the Russian Black Sea ports. The precise reasons for the Ottomans entering the war alongside the Central Powers remain cloudy – entering the war would have dire economic effects for a country that had only recently fought two losing wars in the Balkans. The famous "gift" of two German Navy vessels, the battlecruiser *Goeben* and the light cruiser *Breslau* in August 1914, no doubt

---

[90] Gatrell, *Russia's First World War*, 200, 271.

[91] *Ibid.*, 237; Hubertus F. Jahn, *Patriotic Culture in Russia during World War I* (Cornell University Press, 1995), 174.

was influential, but hardly sufficient cause to bring the Ottomans into the war on its own. The most likely reason is the growing sense of isolation within the Ottoman Court, the Sublime Porte, as former allies Britain and France made common cause with the traditional enemy, Russia. Fueled by effective diplomacy by Germany through the first decade of the twentieth century, the decision to enter the war was, in the opinion of the powerful Minister of War Ismail Enver Pasha, a matter of survival for the Ottoman Caliphate.[92]

Soon after the Ottomans entered the war, the sultan and the chief religious authority in the empire, the Sheykh ul-Islam, issued a *fatwa* invoking a jihad against the primary Entente powers. Accordingly, England, France, and Russia conspired to attack the Islamic Caliphate to continue the long debasement and dismemberment of the Ottoman Empire underway since the eighteenth century. The fatwa served two purposes. The Ottoman political establishment was very well aware of the persuasive power enjoyed by the press. Engaging jihadist rhetoric would enable the state to successfully mobilize reluctant and skeptical constituencies throughout the empire, including Arabs, who had long been agitating for independence.[93] Jihad was also envisioned as an offensive tool to be employed against the Christian empires surrounding the Ottomans. By being issued by the chief religious authority in the Caliphate, the fatwa had the weight of law throughout the Muslim world. The faithful residing in the British, French, and Russian Empires were encouraged to rise up against

---

[92] The Ottoman decision to enter the war on Germany's side was the target of Entente propaganda after the January 1915 publishing of Christiaan Snouck Hurgronje's essay "Holy War Made in Germany." A strong imperialist polemic, the article accused Germany of deliberately provoking jihad to expand the war against Britain and France. Léon Buskens, "Christian Snouck Hurgronje, 'Holy War' and Colonial Concerns, in Erik-Jan Zürcher, *Jihad and Islam in World War I: Studies on the Ottoman Jihad on the Centenary of Snouck Hurgronje's "Holy War Made in Germany"* (Leiden University Press, 2016), 29–51, here 32–33.

[93] Mustafa Aksakal, "The Ottoman Proclamation of Jihad," in Zürcher, *Jihad and Islam in World War I*, 53–69, here 54.

their heathen imperial overlords, and to help carry the Ottoman Empire to victory across North Africa and the Caucasus.

There was a third, unspoken consideration as well. By staking out the argument that the Ottomans were the object of aggression (despite the reality of the unprovoked attack on the Russian ports), the religious and civil authorities were striving to satisfy the conditions for labeling the war as a just conflict according to Islamic law. Not only was this considered crucial to preserving the image of the empire having war forced upon it by its rapacious Christian adversaries. If the Islamic state could be successfully portrayed as being under attack from infidels, military service could be transformed into a religious obligation for every Muslim.[94]

This was no casual exercise. The decision to enter the war was not popular in Istanbul, or other cosmopolitan areas in the Levant, nor in the Arab Crescent. Some saw the fatwa as an ill-advised effort to shoehorn civilian populations who had no cause to take part in a secularized conflict intended to expand the political influence of the Caliphate. Others saw in the decision to go to war the hidden hand of the Germans, who sought to distract the Entente from the pivotal battlegrounds of the Western and Eastern Fronts with the blood of Ottoman volunteers and conscripts. Studiously avoided through the major crises in Libya and the Balkan Wars, by 1914 jihad was a salient tool for mobilizing the people behind the government, even though German military advisors counseled against its use, as it imposed limits on military recruitment to Muslims only.[95]

How successful was the fatwa in practice? Save for a few noteworthy exceptions, primarily the Tuareg uprising against the Italian colonial administration in Libya, very few Muslim subjects in the Entente armies declared neutrality, let alone took up the banner of jihad against their imperial masters. Over a million Muslim soldiers from North Africa and

---

[94] Erik-Jan Zürcher, "Introduction," in Zürcher, *Jihad and Islam in World War I*, 13–27, 14.

[95] The Ottoman decision to enter the war is detailed by Mustafa Aksakal, *The Ottoman Road to War in 1914: The Ottoman Empire and the First World War* (Cambridge University Press, 2008). See also Aksakal, "The Ottoman Proclamation of Jihad," *Jihad and Islam in World War I*, 62–63.

India served in the French and British armies. Anticipated uprisings in Egypt and the Sudan failed to materialize, whereas Bedouin Arabs engaged (with British support) the Turkish Army in a successful insurgency for three years, revealing the rifts between the followers of the Sheykh ul-Islam in Istanbul and the Chief Imam in Mecca. Ottoman military leaders effectively dismissed the internationalist aspects of the jihad pronouncement, seeing its true value residing as a tool to unify disparate non-Arab Muslim communities to defend the empire.

More significantly, jihad enabled the Ottoman Turkish community to engage larger non-Sunni and non-Muslim minorities throughout the empire as enemies of the faith. Years of humiliating defeat at the hands of European neighbors fueled the sense that Christian minorities were dangerous outliers that could, with encouragement, rise up against the empire. The initial targets of Turkish outrage were Greek and Arab Christian communities along the Mediterranean coast. In 1914, the Ottoman Army, with local bands of Turkish civilians, forcibly displaced these groups and removed them from the borders of the empire. This ethnic cleansing was largely bloodless in comparison with the fate awaiting the Armenians residing in Anatolia. Numbering some 1.2 million persons in January 1915, over the course of the next three years, an estimated 800,000 to 900,000 Armenian civilians and conscripts were killed by Turks, Kurds, and other Muslim groups at the direct instruction of the ruling CUP (Committee of Ruling and Progress) party. The justifications for the massacres are thin, including fears that Armenian deserters to the Russian Army were returning home to sow dissension and raise an insurgency against the Ottomans. Such claims concealed a precalculated ambition, linked to earlier genocides in the 1890s, to remove large Christian minorities from the empire, freeing up new land and other property for impoverished Muslims. The slaughter was extensive and brutal. Entire units of Armenian men, called up in October 1914, were marched into the hills and shot. Civilians in villages and small towns were rounded up in the middle of the night and forcibly marched hundreds of miles into the Anatolian desert. There they were set upon by soldiers and Kurdish mobs, who were instructed to leave no one alive. Stripped naked, women and children were killed with bayonets and knives, bullets deemed too expensive to use on them. Once killed, the bodies, stripped of all possessions, were left unburied for scavengers to pick clean. The extent of the Armenian genocide remains disputed today. For years members of the Turkish government and its academic establishment denied it happened, let alone whether it is was included in the October 1914 fatwa announcement proclaiming jihad against the Entente Christian powers. Historians Benny Morris and Dror Ze'evi note the fatwa's existentialist language convinced Ottoman Muslims that Christian minorities were part of the same threat: "The call for holy war also reinforced religious fervor against Ottoman Christians. Though the fatwa did not name internal Christian minorities, many Muslims mentally lumped them together with Russia, Britain, and France."[96] Once jihad was pronounced, the prospect of extreme violence against any perceived threat was inevitable.

The Allied Colonial Armies: Empire and Religion

The Allied reliance upon manpower levied from across their global empires – nearly two million African and Indian soldiers in the British and French armies – introduced unique challenges for all involved when the question of accounting for their religious needs arose; challenges that have been all but ignored in a hundred years of historiography. Indian historian Santana Das poignantly captures this omission when he writes, "These men have been doomed to wander in the no man's land between the Eurocentric narratives of the 'Great war and modern memory' and nationalist histories of India."[97] Das identifies the conundrum surrounding the largely lost narratives of the subalterned colonial soldiers, who have been largely written out of the histories of the war and the independence struggles of the twentieth century.

The silence of memory is particularly acute in questions related to religion and faith. French and British colonial forces were comprised of men from dozens of different ethnic and cultural backgrounds. Martial races

---

[96] Benny Morris and Dror Ze'evi, *The Thirty-Year Genocide: Turkey's Destruction of its Christian Minorities, 1894–1924* (Harvard University Press, 1919), 141–142, 150, 158–160, 244–245, quote on 148.

[97] Santana Das, *India, Empire, and First World War Culture: Writings, Images, and Songs* (Cambridge University Press 2018), 16.

ideology restricted military service to specific groups in North Africa and India, largely those that had proved the most supportive in the consolidation of imperial control. In British India, this translated into an army comprised almost entirely of Muslim Pathans and Punjabis, Sikhs, and Gurkhas.[98] In many cases before and during the war, religion was employed by the British as a subordinate test of martial prowess and suitability for military service. Recruitment appeals made by the local princes explicitly aligned religious and caste identity with military service, arguing that loyalty to the empire fulfilled obligations of faith held in common among Kshatriya Hindus, Muslims, and Sikhs.[99]

The French recruited over 450,000 Algerian, Senegalese, Moroccan, Tunisian, Malagasies, and Somali soldiers over four years. The necessity of raising a colonial army had long since been accepted by the French high command; *la force noire* was intended to make up for a declining metropolitan birth rate in the event of war with Germany. Colonial administrators and politicians, conversely, justified the levy as a deeply racist cultural exchange. "Republican ideals and a sense of racial superiority underpinned the French 'civilizing mission,' which would raise up the cultural level of colonized peoples. Military service was part of this. This 'school of the nation' would inculcate French ideals in recruits, who paid a 'blood tax' in return for the benefits of French rule."[100] Despite the lingering image of French tolerance born in the trench community, Muslim French North African and Senegalese troops were never fully trusted by their commanders. Battalions and regiments were amalgamated with metropolitan units. Colonials who were promoted to officers (lieutenants and captains) were never put in command of white troops.[101]

---

[98] Vedica Kant, *"If I Die Here, Who Will Remember Me?" India and the First World War* (Roli Books, 2014), 27.

[99] Das, *India, Empire, and First World War Culture*, 47.

[100] Richard S. Fogarty, *Race and War in France: Colonial Subjects in the French Army, 1914–1918* (Johns Hopkins University Press, 2012), 60–62, 66–68, 71–72.

[101] Christian Koller, "Colonial Military Participation in Europe (Africa)," *1914–1918 Online: International Encyclopedia of the First World War*. https://encyclopedia.1914-1918-online.net/article/colonial_military_participation_in_europe_africa Accessed June 7, 2020.

The experience of engaging in a war far from home and so removed from their own cultures and societies encouraged many African and Indian soldiers to embrace their religious identities. This was not so much a case of soldiers seeking a cleaner and purer connection with their faith as perhaps an attempt to find normalcy in the midst of horrific war. Certainly such wartime devotion was no different from the experiences of European soldiers, who similarly clung to their Christian faiths as a moral shield while under fire. After experiencing first-hand the tremendous killing power of industrialized war at Ypres or Verdun, Muslims, Hindus, and Sikhs alike fell back onto familiar eschatological language to contextualize their own sense of futility under fire. Muslim soldiers contextualized the war through reference to the 680 CE battle of Karbala, which set in motion the events causing the doctrinal split between Sunni and Shia Muslims. Hindus and Sikhs consistently referenced the Mahabharata, an epic text describing war between two cousins that nearly consumed their families. In both cases, the awesome killing forces employed in Europe defied any other rational contextualization. The conflict too was perceived by non-Europeans as a fratricidal contest, a family war that would consume everybody and everything in its path.[102]

The possibility of an Ottoman jihad and its potential disruptive effect on colonial Muslim soldiers was treated seriously by the British and French. The question of divided loyalties and the prospect of open mutiny compelled the French to refrain from deploying North African regiments in the 1915 Dardanelles campaign. Manpower constraints and the government's emphasis on prosecuting the war in Flanders left the British little choice but to employ Indian regiments in Mesopotamia. The expeditionary force commanded by Major General Charles V. F. Townshend that was compelled to surrender to the Ottoman Army at Kut al-Amara in April 1916, after a 147 day siege, was made up largely of Indian soldiers, many of them Muslims. By the end of the war, over 124,000 Indian troops were employed in Mesopotamia, along with another 115,000 laborers. For all of this, the incidents of insubordination and mutiny on religious grounds were relatively few. Between January 1915 and February 1916, three regimental sized

---

[102] Kant, *"If I Die Here,"* 169–170.

incidents affected Muslim Indian units that were ordered to Mesopotamia. More likely were individual cases of desertion by soldiers who experienced doubts over fighting their coreligionists; but even here, the numbers were relatively light. The overwhelming number of Muslims in the Indian Expeditionary Force remained loyal to the British crown.[103]

Conclusion

Conventional perspectives hold that the world's great faiths were, with only a few notable exceptions, repulsed by the First World War. Entreaties to stop the violence were met with open skepticism by the participating governments, which were blinded to the scale of the immoral crime that was the war. Despite their best attempts, the community of faith was not only unable to stem to bloodshed, they were confined to the roles of bolstering morale and assuaging grief.

Not surprisingly, the assumption was far from the mark. In nation after nation, the primary response by virtually all of the mainstream and ancillary religious faiths and denominations was to present a united front with national secular political authority. Calls to peace and rejecting war were the outlier responses, and those who issued them were greeted with hostility and skepticism, regardless of their status and authority. Lesser ecumenical and theological authorities rejected peace plans and offers of arbitration, choosing to align their influence and authority with the nation in arms. Such acts were pursued as much out of the desire for personal and denomination-wide influence in the public sphere of politics and policy. Western European Catholic, Protestant, and Jewish hierarchies embraced the First World War as a great opportunity to improve their respective status in their home communities.

---

[103] *Ibid.*, 196–197; Fogarty, *Race and War in France*, 170, 196; Gökhan Çetinsaya, "Kut al-Amara," *1914–1918 Online: International Encyclopedia of the First World War.* https://encyclopedia.1914-1918-online.net/article/kut_al-amara Accessed June 7, 2020; Kaushik Roy, *Indian Army and the First World War, 1914–1918* (Oxford University Press, 2018), https://books.google.com/books?id=rVZxDwAAQBAJ&printsec=frontcover&source=gbs_ge_summary_r&cad=0#v=onepage&q&f=false Accessed June 7, 2020.

Furthermore, casting the war as a liminal secular moment, the point when the legitimate authority of organized religion in daily life was challenged by reason, irony, and skepticism, obscures how tightly entwined religious and national identities were. The calls to arms across Europe and in the United States were imbued with a sacred character that was familiar in its fervor, expressing the desires of people to be part of a righteous society in war. Political and faith leaders acted in concert to promote national mobilization as an exercise in unity, framing the conflict as a just and good contest to preserve the secular and religious commonwealth. The obverse of this interaction is the ease with which faith communities acquiesced in the legitimization of violence, not only against the external enemy, but against suspect minorities within as well. Militant narratives of obligation and total subordination to the will of the state left little room for equivocation or debate over moral proportionality. Wartime governments and bureaucracies brooked no dissent that affected the prosecution of the war. Legal coercive policies could be and were strengthened by appeals to solidarity on the basis of faith. In extreme cases – Russia, the Ottoman Empire, Austria-Hungary – this translated into legitimized internal violence against minority religious communities. This last point remains the most problematic. Not only does it betray consensus narratives arguing for a weakening of the relationship between religion and the state, these types of radically violent action undertaken to create a homogenous community identity became increasingly normalized over the twentieth century. Contrary to the expectations of its critics after the First World War, religion has become even more firmly entrenched in national identity across much of the globe.

2 Faith in the Trenches

For decades, the primary historiographic trend addressing religion and the First World War has centered on the response of church hierarchies at home and in the field, according to Annette Becker. Writing about the French Catholic establishment, she may well be speaking for other nations and denominations when she states, "of the Catholic 'trilogy' – the papacy, the clerics, and the faithful – only the first two aspects have been much

explored."[104] While her verdict may fall short of the mark in some cases –
the questions of faith and the war have been considered more carefully in
studies of conscientious objectors in the United States and the United
Kingdom, for example – overall it is accurate. Perhaps this is because the
question of faith is so personal and taken for granted. Maybe its treatment
by scholars reflects an inherent bias against a subject so intangible and
unquantifiable by traditional archival methods. Either way, traditional
histories of the war have, at least until the late 1980s, ignored completely
the question of faith, even as they account for the position of the Protestant
and Catholic establishments in each combatant state.

The personal faith of the combatants, and the measures the state
employed to bolster their morale, are explored in this section. Personal
belief systems and folk tradition that were mobilized by the private soldier
are considered, as well as the various supernatural narratives used to
contextualize the many encounters with mortality they faced. Chaplains
are examined at large and in some specific detail, offering a glimpse into
their tremendous responsibilities and how they were perceived by the rank
and file. Finally, the question of dissent, and the measures employed by the
state against men of conscience in an attempt to force compliance with the
war effort, is examined.

Superstition, Faith, and the Common Soldier

For soldiers from all sides, the encounter with the war was a deeply personal
and spiritual affair. Individual civilians *cum* soldiers were ill-equipped to
emotionally contextualize the constant reminders of mortality the surrounded them. In the trenches, soldiers lived with death. Surrounded by
rotting corpses and living in a shattered landscape, the futility of their own
personal struggles to stay alive was a constant worry. Survival could be
utterly random. Thousands died daily in what the British called "wastage" –
the standard attrition of men from snipers, artillery "stonks," and small
raids. No one was safe, anyone could die at any time and be called to
account for their actions in the afterlife. Add to this the very real sanctions

---

[104] Annette Becker, *War and Faith: The Religious Imagination in France, 1914–1930*
(Berg, 1998), 2–3.

against taking human life that are central to the Judeo-Christian tradition. While doctrine and hierarchies may have settled the question of just war and the act of necessary killing, the factory worker and peasant believer were not so readily absolved of their own guilt over taking the lives of the enemy.[105] If taking a life was a mortal sin, how were they to reconcile killing dozens of the enemy? Another consideration was the weight of the petty venal sins accompanying life away from home and family. For the faithful, life in wartime was not just a matter of survival, it also was a daily test of their commitment to God. From dealing with petty gossips and thieves to resisting the impulse to visit sanctioned brothels or *estaminets*, the drumbeat of constant temptation only added to the emotional stress for many.

It is thus little surprise that many soldiers turned to personal tokens and expressions of divine intercession. These ranged from superstitions and fetishes, to oft-repeated accounts of direct spiritual intervention on behalf of the faithful in crisis, to narratives of redemption and the ever-constant bargains for life in exchange for a promise of future moral conduct. In the face of death and physical annihilation, the embrace of the supernatural by soldiers reveals how thin the veneer of rationality was on Western society. Under dire stress for prolonged periods of time, even the most reason-minded men discovered a degree of security in fantastical rumors and stories. At the start of the war, reports of miracles spread throughout the ranks. British, Commonwealth, and French soldiers alike described encountering shattered churches, where all save the crucifix, or the statues of the Virgin Mary and Christ Child, was utterly destroyed. The surviving icons however were completely untouched, as if they were protected by some sort of divine force from shrapnel and debris.[106] Such accounts were not dissimilar to those about the ruined steeple of the Basilica de Notre-Dame

---

[105] More recently, critics of just war theory have concluded the quest to apply moral limitations on war to be a failed effort, historically adapted to reconcile inconsistencies within early Christian doctrine regarding war and state coercive force. See Robert Meagher, *Killing from the Inside Out: Moral Injury and Just War* (Cascade Books, 2014), 129–131.

[106] Alan Wilkinson, *The Church of England and the First World War*. Third Edition (The Lutterworth Press, 1978, 1996, 2014), 195; Becker, *War and Faith*, 97;

de Brebières, the site of the much-rumored "Golden Virgin." So long as the statue of the Virgin and Child remained intact, the war would continue; but, in a twist, the side that destroyed it would soon thereafter lose the war.[107] Such outlandish tales should not be dismissed out of hand as wishful thinking or as propaganda. Rather, they speak toward the need within the ranks for some sign of divine favor that could in turn be translated as proof that God did care about individual soldiers. Miracles were evidence that, amidst such a total and devastating war, single lives did matter and were worth protecting.

An extension of the miracle accounts were the more fantastic stories of the dead rising or appearing unexpectedly in battle to warn or protect those they encounter from imminent danger. These accounts are not to be confused with the stories of spiritual intervention; rather the actors are usually presented as casualties of the current war, in some cases recognizable to the living as recently deceased comrades.[108] Again, while tempting to classify these accounts as a crude form of propaganda intended more for domestic civilian consumption than for the soldiers in the field, there are cultural and folklore precedents for these reports. One of the oldest mythic tropes in Western Europe was built around the prospect of the "returning dead." Accordingly communities and individual peasants and travelers would encounter the deceased as they set out to complete unfinished business. These were not merely animated corpses, but in the accounts were capable of reason and could – and did – converse with the living.[109]

Far more common among soldiers from all sides was the desire to carry some sort of talisman or object to keep death at bay. Many of these objects

Jay Winter, *Sites of Memory, Sites of Mourning: The Great War in European Cultural History* (Cambridge University Press, 1995), 66.

[107] "Item MM 120129, Photograph "Basilica of Notre-Dame de Brebières," Albert, France, Sergeant John Lord, World War I, 1916. Museums Victoria Collections. https://collections.museumvictoria.com.au/items/1703721 Accessed November 4, 2019.

[108] Winter, *Sites of Memory*, 66–67, 68–69.

[109] Nancy Mandeville Caciola, *Afterlives: The Return of the Dead in the Middle Ages* (Cornell University Press, 2017), 125–136.

were religious in nature, even if the wielder was not particularly devout or observant. Pocket Bibles or books of prayer were popular among Protestants and Catholics; even if they weren't read, their mere presence was held to be a good omen. Many Catholic soldiers took to carrying rosaries and scapulars, convinced these artifacts would protect the wearer from harm. And for all soldiers, mass-produced religious medals also came into their own. First adopted by Catholics, who were served by a robust industry dedicated to mass-producing trinkets and symbols of personal devotion, medallions dedicated to various saints and the Virgin Mary were often given by family members hoping the talisman would preserve their loved ones. Some of the medals acquired a more universal appeal, as the prevalence of Saint Christopher medallions would show. Perhaps rivalled only by crucifixes, these small medals were worn universally by Catholics and Protestants alike, revealing the ecumenical sensibilities of the soldier in the trenches.[110]

In the East, Russian soldiers were committed to the practice of carrying holy icons to the front. Following examples from earlier conflicts, including the 1904 war with Japan, Orthodox bishops blessed entire regiments, carrying the icons from their cathedrals before the men as a sign of devotion and favor.[111] Confidence placed in religious iconography extended to the

---

[110] Philip Jenkins, *The Great and Holy War: How World War I Became a Religious Crusade* (HarperOne, 2015), 123–124; Stéphene Audoin-Rouzeau and Annette Becker, *14–18: Understanding the Great War* (Hill and Wang, 2002), 132–134; Becker, *War and Faith*, 99–103; Patrick J. Houlihan, *Catholicism and the Great War: Religion and Everyday Life in Germany and Austria-Hungary, 1914–1922* (Cambridge University Press, 2017), 133,144–148; Richard Schweitzer, *The Cross and the Trenches: Religious Faith and Doubt Among British and American Great War Soldiers* (Praeger Publishers, 2003), 28; Owen Davies, *A Supernatural War: Magic, Divination, and Faith during the First World War* (Oxford University Press, 2019), 177–217.

[111] Betsy Perabo, *Russian Orthodoxy and the Russo-Japanese War* (Bloomsbury Academic, 2017), 106–107, 129–130; Robert L. Nichols, "Nicholas II and the Russian Icon," in Jefferson J. A. Gatrall and Douglas Greenfield, *Alter Icons: The Russian Icon and Modernity* (The Pennsylvania State University Press, 2010), 74–88.

manufacture and release of propaganda prints, not only in Russia, but by all combatants as well. The subjects and their activity varied widely. Of course depictions of Christ, the Virgin Mary, and angels were common (as were, conversely, images of the enemy in league or conversation with Satan or other diabolical agents). Similarly, known religious or historical figures, presumed to have been elevated to sainthood (or its equivalent for secular historical figures), appear in popular prints as icons of reverence and inspiration. A noteworthy example is an American print commissioned from the Chicago publisher Charles Gustrine. Entitled "True Sons of Freedom," it presents an attack by African American soldiers on a German trench, blessed by the spirit of Abraham Lincoln, who is portrayed looking down upon the incident from above. Heavy-handed, indeed; yet it is of a type with other images of Madonnas, Virgins, Mariannes, and Christs blessing the masses.[112] Yet another type of image charged with religious significance portrays soldiers and civilians in the act of humble devotion. Often reproduced with a prayer, such prints were intended as an invocation of support, favor, and supplication – they also infer the subordination of the private religious sphere to the demands of the public state.

Another form of supernatural intercession that appears largely in the postwar historiography is the timely appearance of ghostly apparitions. Soldiers in an untenable position would be rescued by the arrival of a ghostly host, at times led or accompanied by winged angels. Unlike the accounts of appearance of recently dead soldiers, here the rescuers were clearly supernatural. The most famous was the appearance of a host of angels, led by a golden-haired St. George, during the August 1914 British retreat from Mons. Soon after, similar accounts of divine intervention were accredited to Jeanne D'Arc during the German advance in the month-long Battle of the Marne, and later her appearance in French propaganda at the

---

[112] Robert Cozzolino, Anne Classen Knutson, and David M. Lubin, *World War I and American Art* (Pennsylvania Academy of the Fine Arts and Princeton University Press, 2016), 186; Karen Petrone, *The Great War in Russian Memory* (Indiana University Press, 2011), 34–36.

bomb-damaged cathedral at Reims.[113] Alleged spiritual and divine interventions were also accredited to the Russian Army in 1914, in the form of the ghost of General Mikhail Skobelev, the "White General" and hero of the 1877 Russo-Turkish War. Clad in his white uniform and astride a white horse, the ghostly general reportedly appeared in the night before Russian pickets on the eve of battle. The Virgin Mary herself was reported to have put in an appearance prior to the October 1914 engagement at Augustovo, appearing again before the encampment's guards to point the way westward toward victory.[114] All these cases were fictionalized creations, following the September 29, 1914 publication of Arthur Machen's fantastical short story, "The Bowmen," in the *London Evening News*. The introduction of a host of ghostly longbowmen, evoking the 1415 Battle of Agincourt, as the saviors of a near-defeated British Expeditionary Force during the long retreat from Mons was far more popular than Machen could have ever guessed. Despite his efforts to reveal the fictional origins of the account, it quickly passed into the public memory as an authentic narrative. Soon many across England claimed they had heard of the story from an acquaintance or friend, who had heard it themselves from another friend who had learned of it from a veteran "who was there." The spiritual intercession narrative virtually disappears after 1915.[115]

Miracles, talismans, and new myth-making aside, the question remains of how soldiers on either side of the conflict reconciled their war and their faith. Consider the reputation of British soldiers in peacetime. If asked, casual observers might fall back on the admonishment of Field Marshal

---

[113] Jennifer Kilgore, "Joan of Arc as Propaganda Motif from the Dreyfus Affair to the Second World War," *Revue LISA: Littératures, histoire des Idées, Images et Sociétés du monde Anglophone.* VI:1 (2008): Propagating Ideas and Images. https://journals.openedition.org/lisa/519 Accessed October 14, 2019; David Clarke, "Rumours of Angels: A Legend of the First World War," *Folklore.* 113:2 (October 2002), 151–173, 152.

[114] Ralph Shirley, *The Angel Warriors at Mons* (Newspaper Publicity Co., 1915) 10–11.

[115] See David Clarke, *The Angel of Mons: Phantom Soldiers and Ghostly Guardians* (Wiley, 2004).

Arthur Wellesley, First Duke of Wellington, that the private soldiers in his army were "the scum of the earth."[116] Comprised of vile, ill-bred, and desperate men, Napoleonic era British soldiers were a dangerous lot, certain to corrupt any young men of character who came into their fold. Not all fell into this category though. Even in the early nineteenth century, British soldiers were targets of evangelical missionaries at home garrison and abroad. Initially resisted by officers, such efforts were quickly institutionalized through the creation of the chaplaincy as the conversion experience improved discipline and had a marked impact on drunkenness in the other ranks. Yet it would be a mistake to assign full credit for the spread of religiosity in the ranks just before and during the war. The peacetime army, including the Territorial Force, reflected the values and beliefs of the communities from which its recruits were drawn. While there was little patience offered for the most overtly devoted faithful in the barracks, the hazing they experienced should not be taken as evidence of a hostile anti-religious mass response to these (often self-described) Christian soldiers. Rather many enlisted men rejected not the spirit of Christianity, but the open and quite conscious overt display of religious conduct.[117] The entire ritual of earnest Christian observance – foreswearing drink, profanity, and grumbling – was seen as an attempt to lord over one's peers, to show officers that they were somehow better than the rank and file, and deserved special concessions. This was in turn considered a marked act of disrespect toward the men they served with. The hazing that ensued was intended to reinforce the egalitarian ethos of the barracks.

Within the French Army, the question of reconciling war and faith was more nuanced than peacetime trends would have indicated. Anticlericalism did not necessarily translate into mass agnosticism. Where the general motivations and conduct of the local parish priest were frequent targets of satire and scorn, most Frenchmen, urban and rural alike, retained

[116] Richard Holmes, *Tommy: The British Soldier on the Western Front, 1914–1918* (Harper Collins, 2004), 118.

[117] Michael Snape, *The Redcoat and Religion: The Forgotten History of the British Soldier from the Age of Marlborough to the Eve of the First World War* (Routledge, 2005), 178.

a persistent faith that defied secularist trends. How did this translate into action in the trenches? The scale of death and destruction was so massive during the war, many sought refuge in religious idiom and ritual to contextualize the battlefield and the frequency of violent death. As Leonard V. Smith observes, Catholicism was particularly well-suited for constructing narratives of the transcendence of the soul in the face of physical annihilation. Numerous soldiers came to view the prospect of death in battle as a sort of martyrdom for God and the French community. The suffering of the trenches was compared to that of Christ on the way to crucifixion. Assisted by the fervent imaginations of priests serving alongside other men in the trenches, a conviction grew that the immediate challenges and obstacles of wartime prepared the *poilu* for the ultimate act of sacrifice that would lead to a better future France, a better future world.[118] The act of rendering this perfect sacrifice was also presented as a reenactment of the life and death of Christ. Through this *imitatio Christi* device, brave soldiers who did not shirk from their obligation were guaranteed a place in heaven even as their bodies remained alarmingly vulnerable. Death was not to be feared; rather, it brought one closer to God and their ultimate reward. Yet, Smith notes, even doubt had a place in the religious imagination of the front. Personal fears and doubts were only natural; indeed, many compared their own fears with the anguish of Christ at Gethsemane and during crucifixion. The key was not to allow doubt to unseat one's commitment to the war. No one could guess as to what tangible earthly outcome their death would contribute. Death and sacrifice might not even prove sufficient to win the war. But then, perhaps the temporal suffering of the war was part of a larger plan to make more manifest God's plan for all humanity.[119]

Divided largely along two lines – Catholicism and Lutheranism – the Christians of the German Army followed widely diverging paths of belief. Prior to the war, Protestantism was the dominant faith in the Army, albeit one with steadily declining influence. Church parades and the ensuing sermons were seen as a distraction by many, or as an annoying obstruction

---

[118] Leonard V. Smith, *The Embattled Self: French Soldiers' Testimony of the Great War* (Cornell University Press, 2007), 63–64.

[119] *Ibid.*, 64–67.

to a drill- and work-free Sunday. Protestant chaplains were more likely to embrace the Christian nationalist message, expounding on the religious obligation of German soldiers to deliver victory through their own actions and, if necessary, sacrifice. Such a message might prove amenable in the opening months of the war. As the conflict settled into a vicious long-term struggle, one in which the German Army was consistently outnumbered and compelled to accept horrific casualties, even Protestant chaplains found the nationalistic message hard to swallow. Concepts like "noble sacrifice" and "holy cause" sounded empty in the context of Verdun and the Somme; how many noble sacrifices were necessary to satisfy the whims of a distant and apparently bloodthirsty God, in the quest for victory?[120]

German and Austrian Catholics, on the other hand, appear to have found their faith to be quite resilient in the face of modern industrialized warfare. Catholicism's ongoing relationship with supernatural intercession in the form of visitations, apparitions, and miracles, along with the panoply of saints and the continued veneration of their earthly remains as a testament of their proximity to God, rendered it more adaptable to the circumstances of trench warfare. Ritual offered comfort that no Protestant service could approximate. Amulets and scapulae were tangible symbols of God's favor. The fine line between faith and magical thinking was blurred during the war, providing tangible benefits to believers.[121]

On the whole, however, the majority of soldiers do appear to have shared a common desire to live and express their religious sentiment with minimal attention – a live-and-let-live sort of exchange, in which soldiers didn't ask questions or make assumptions about their bunkmate's religious observations. To a degree, this forbearance matched up well with existing civilian constraints around discussing politics and religion at home. It was only natural that this informal ecumenicalism took root in the barracks and trenches. The war's totality negated prior mandates toward religious privilege and exceptionalism among regiments. In countries with no preponderant declaration of faith – Great Britain, Germany, the United States –

[120] David Stone, *The Kaiser's Army: The German Army in World War One* (Conway/Bloomsbury, 2015), 188–189.

[121] Houlihan, *Catholicism and the Great War*, 119–120.

regiments were increasingly comprised of men from all denominations and confessions. And in those where religious identity was more uniform – France, Austria-Hungary, Italy, and Russia – devotion was matched with pragmatic skepticism. Overall, religion sustained all of those men who sought refuge under its broad tent, be they devout true believers or fair-weather apostates, for as long as they sought it. As Adrian Gregory notes, "Should the First World War be seen as a great war of religion? The answer is a frustrating yes and no." At the highest level of social contextualization of the war, that is to say between combatant populations and their religious and civil leaders, religion was a critical force by which to lay out the context and conduct of the war. In this way, the First World War was driven and affected deeply by religion. At the individual level, however, religion was supplemented by something less tangible and absolute. Faith was a deeply personal matter. Capable of accommodating skepticism or superstition, it was always unique to the personal outlook, yet also unifying in that it gave shape and form to how one fit into the larger picture, not merely on the battlefield, but the hereafter as well. As Gregory notes, of course the idea of "wartime religion" has its limits, "[b]ut we also need to acknowledge that religious practices, language, and imagery were intimately engaged in making sense of 'war experience.'"[122]

Underlying these issues of faith in crisis is the question of how combat and the war at large represented a "second chance" for the individual soldier and the communities within which he resided. The experience of surviving near misses that maimed or killed neighboring soldiers, some of them friends and even family, were sometimes hard to rationalize. For those men who were religious or spiritual in sentiment, their close shave with death represented a chance at recovering or preserving a damaged or distressed faith. Redemption was not restricted to the individual. With the war dragging on, congregations at home and at the front saw it as a great test of faith. And on the larger stage, civic and religious leaders combined

---

[122] Adrian Gregory, "Beliefs and Religion," in Jay Winter, ed., *The Cambridge History of The First World War*. Volume III: *Civil Society* (Cambridge University Press, 2014), 418–444, here 443.

their efforts to present a message of the war being a great test of faith, a chance to experience national redemption in the eyes of God.

Not all military historians have been susceptible to this narrative trope, however. Individuals working primarily on the social history of the soldier in wartime present more nuanced outlooks on the war and its effects on religious sentiment. In his study of the American doughboy, for example, Richard S. Faulkner identifies a duality of belief that weighs on the fulcrum of combat circumstance and experience. There first is the nonbeliever or skeptic who experiences a "foxhole conversion" moment. Such moments featured in many wartime narratives and memoirs, enabling such tropes to assume the character of normalcy. Chaplains, soldiers, and aid workers sharing accounts of battlefield conversions created the perception that this was the more common experience among soldiers facing death, but a closer examination of many individual experiences reveals a *quid pro quo*. Caught under fire, the individual soldier makes a bargain with God – the "save me now and I will serve you later" exchange. For such men, their secular or lackadaisical frame of reference when it comes to faith is overwhelmed by the prospect of mortality, leading them to offer a trade with the divine.[123]

Battlefield conversions were not limited to peacetime agnostics. The totality of suffering at the front revealed for some the depths of God's mercy. Abandoned to their fate by the cruelty of men, they found spiritual purpose in the war. Seeking a way to express this newfound faith, many turned to Catholicism. As Stéphene Audoin-Rouzeau and Annette Becker note, "it was also the specific nature of Catholicism, the religion of miracle, that drove people to conversion. The conversion experiences were both responses to God's miracles and miracles in themselves."[124] Thus the war becomes a redemptive miracle, an opportunity for new believers to achieve grace in the moment before their physical annihilation and ensuing judgment before God.

Alternatively there was the collapse of faith under fire. Men who had lived genuinely Christian lives before the war, often emphasizing Christ's

---

[123] Richard Faulkner, *Pershing's Crusaders: The American Soldier in World War I* (University Press of Kansas, 2017), 412–414.

[124] Audoin-Rouzeau and Becker, *14–18*, 127–128.

messages of love and charity, found their entire belief system shattered by the horrific destructive power the war brought to bear. Immersed in the constant death and devastation of the trenches, such men felt abandoned by their God, forsaken and condemned to the troughs of despair. Comparing the two tropes, it is clear that it is the combat experience that transcends existing belief and faith, triggering an opposing reaction to existing value frameworks that define the self.[125]

Chaplaincy

Considered as a whole, the chaplains of the different armies, while divided by national and sectarian identities, were remarkably similar. British chaplains focused on how their nation's mission was not only to defend their allies in the field, but also to help safeguard the Christian virtues of the nation in trench and encampment. From the start of the war, Anglican and Presbyterian ministers volunteered in great numbers to serve as uniformed guardians of the volunteers making up Kitchener's "New Army." They were joined by nonconformists – Baptists, Congregationalists, Wesleyans, and Methodists – in smaller numbers. Recruitment among British clergy was wholly voluntary; given that the individual candidate was in good health and morally sound, they were welcomed in service. Recruitment initially was brisk, putting some communities in the position of having to bring retired clergymen back to the civilian pulpit while younger ministers answered the call to service. By war's end over 5,000 clergymen from nearly a dozen denominations and from all across the globe were commissioned as chaplains.[126]

Prior to joining the war, the United States' military establishment considered the uniformed chaplaincy an essential safeguard for the morality of its soldiers and sailors. Progressive policy makers throughout the federal government reasoned that without the paternal guidance offered by chaplains, young servicemen would fall victim to the many immoral temptations surrounding their bases and ports of call. As Edward Waggoner

---

[125] Faulkner, *Pershing's Crusaders*, 414–415.

[126] Edward Madigan and Michael Snape, *The Clergy in Khaki: New Perspectives on British Army Chaplaincy in the First World War* (Routledge, 2016), 2.

described, "the chaplain's primary duty was to help sailors [and soldiers] grow up – using personal example, sympathy, and military rank and title to influence them toward good behavior."[127] In practice, however, such preferences were consistently underfulfilled as the United States hurriedly mobilized for war. The American Expeditionary Force suffered a shortage of chaplains throughout the entire war. In 1917, the army (including the National Guard) could barely muster 100 chaplains in service, and many of these were of the Protestant denominations. In late 1918, when the AEF consisted of over two million men, it remained short 420 chaplains, even after General John J. Pershing authorized the commissioning of enlisted men and civilian aid workers who could pass an evaluation board examination on their pastoral and general educational knowledge.[128] By October 1918, 789 chaplains were in service. Over 86 percent were assigned to combat arms units (infantry, artillery, cavalry, engineers), leaving 105 to counsel soldiers in the rear echelon (including base and general hospitals).[129]

The French position on chaplains was complicated by the Third Republic's tenuous relationship with the Catholic Church before the war. In 1880 the position of military chaplain was banned as part of the rising anticlerical tide following the Franco-Prussian War. In 1889 the government granted clergymen one year's noncombatant uniformed service. The Church's ability to resist the new laws was limited; years of anti-Republican activities and the general low perception of the clergy undermined any hope for reversing the policies.[130] Not until May 5, 1913 were chaplains authorized in time of war, but only on a 1:1,000 ratio of priests to enlisted men. As a result, only 1,500 clergymen were recruited during the war to serve as chaplains. These were scattered in penny-packets throughout the army. The line establishment received about half of the official chaplains. The remainder were posted to the medical services, assigned primarily to hospitals.

---

[127] Edward Waggoner, *Religion in Uniform: A Critique of US Military Chaplaincy* (Lexington Books, 2019), 16.

[128] Faulkner, *Pershing's Crusaders*, 417–419. [129] *Ibid.*, 421.

[130] Anita Rasi May, *Patriot Priests: French Catholic Clergy and National Identity in World War I* (University of Oklahoma Press, 2018), 18–20.

Despite the *Union sacrée*, the civilian government remained skeptical of the allegiances of clergymen in the army. Unlike her Protestant allies, France never exempted priests from military service. As a result, over 32,000 clergymen, including monks and seminary students, entered the army during the war, with many of them serving as infantrymen. As a result, much of the need for spiritual guidance among the rank and file was met by their own comrades, priest-*poilus* who attended to their fellow soldiers independently of the established chaplaincy.[131]

French military anticlericalism was matched in sentiment and practice by the Italian Army. In fact, Italy set the example for France to follow, having by 1878 mandated clerical military service and abolishing the chaplaincy in the military. In 1911, the government allowed volunteer priests to serve as chaplains in the army's medical services in Libya. As Italy entered the war in 1915, every regiment was assigned a chaplain. Overall the Italian Army was served by 2,400 military chaplains, while some 15,000 clergy were conscripted into service. Most of the latter were assigned to the medical services, while seminarians were dispatched directly to line branch units. The work of the chaplains was supplemented by a wide range of volunteer evangelical Catholic activities, ranging from the distribution of religious newspapers, books, Bibles, and material necessities.[132] Even more significant were the ninety-six *Case di soldato* – "Soldier's Homes" – sponsored by the Church as a counter to perceived socialist influences among soldiers. These hostel-styled venues provided places for soldiers to

---

[131] May, *Patriot Priests*, 33; Becker, *War and Faith*, 32–33.

[132] Maria Paiano, "Religious Mobilization and Popular Belief (Italy)," *1914–1918 Online: International Encyclopedia of the First World War*. https://encyclopedia.1914-1918-online.net/article/religious_mobilization_and_popular_belief_italy Accessed October 19, 2018; Maria Paiano, "Italian Jesuits and the Great War: Chaplains and Priest-Soldiers of the Province of Rome," *Journal of Jesuit Studies* 4 (2017), 637–657, here 638–639; Carlo Stiaccini, "The Catholic Church and the War," in Vanya Wilcox, *Italy in the Era of the Great War*. History of Warfare, Volume 120 (Brill, 2018), 272–287, here 279–280.

read, write letters, enjoy a hot meal and entertainment, and otherwise gain a short respite from the war.[133]

One aspect of the close relationship between Russia's Orthodox Synod and the Romanov dynasty was the early integration of the clergy within the army. Since 1800, provisions were made for military chaplains in the Imperial Russian Army. By 1911, this had grown from a system of regimental chaplains into a much larger and more comprehensive system under the direction of a special protopresbyter (equivalent to an archbishop) of all chaplains appointed directly by Tsar Nicholas II. By the end of 1915, over two thousand chaplains were registered in the army. Predominantly Eastern Orthodox, they also included Jewish rabbis, Catholic and Protestant priests, and imams.[134] The two chief duties of Russian Army chaplains were religious instruction and bolstering morale among the enlisted ranks. Holy icons were brought to the front by direct order of the tsar, where they were used to bless weapons and men alike. Chaplains were expected to provide constant reminders of Russia' goals for the war, echoing the regime's own wartime propaganda. Indeed chaplains frequently exceeded this mandate, going on to promote war as a panacea for all that was wrong in prewar Russian society: "They tried to demonstrate that peace time engenders in people cowardice, 'crude, self-serving egoism,' and 'intellectual stagnation.' War on the other hand arouses the nation, people return from the field of battle 'with a more tempered character, with more patience and confidence in themselves.'"[135]

When the revolutions of 1917 began, the church initially supported Nicholas II and the monarchy, calling as late as February 25 for all Orthodox clergy to surround the throne in its defense. Yet after the revolution, the clergy quickly accepted its verdict. David R. Stone reports that after the March 1917 revolution, the provisional government enlisted chaplains to help boost morale in the battered army. This mission was

---

[133] John Gooch, *The Italian Army and the First World War* (Cambridge University Press, 2014), 164.

[134] Aleksandr Senin, "Russian Army Chaplains During World War I," *Russian Studies in History*. 32:2 (Fall 1993), 43–52, here 43–45.

[135] *Ibid.*, 47–48, quote on 47.

adopted enthusiastically by clergymen who saw it as an opportunity to promote greater adherence to Orthodoxy. As events soured, the largely conservative chaplaincy was increasingly marginalized as part of the problem by soldiers who were tired of the war. Here the clergy were viewed as a catalyst for more useless suffering and death, not as a voice of spiritual guidance to redemption in the face of the personal Calvary brought on by war.[136]

According to Patrick J. Houlihan, efforts to establish a precise reckoning of the number of chaplains in the German and Austro-Hungarian armies are imprecise. Part of the problem is the frequently ad hoc method of recruiting chaplains in the face of modern conscription. Particularly in the Austrian military, the chaplaincy was essentially an afterthought in the larger institutional bureaucracy. Exacerbating the problem is the absence of official records from the German and Austrian establishments, the relevant archives being collateral damage of the Second World War. Houlihan presents an incomplete reckoning, identifying 1,441 chaplains attached to the Prussian establishment, and an unverified tally of 3,077 chaplains in the Austro-Hungarian military. But he concludes that in both cases, "the number of chaplains and military religious caregivers was hazy and indeterminate at best."[137]

In the Ottoman Army, the spiritual needs of the enlisted men and officers were attended to by a cadre of military imams who served the same role as chaplains in the Western militaries. The Ottomans had an equally long and rich tradition of established religious figures in the military, going back at least to the late eighteenth century. As the Ottoman army modernized

---

[136] *Ibid.*, 49; David R. Stone, *The Russian Army in the Great War: The Eastern Front, 1914–1917* (University Press of Kansas, 2015), 282–283.

[137] Houlihan, *Catholicism and the Great War*, 79. Marsha Rozenblit notes the Habsburg Army commissioned 78 rabbis as chaplains by the end of the war, a number insufficient to meet the needs of the 325,000 Jewish soldiers and officers mobilized over the course of the war. Marsha Rozenblit, *Reconstructing a National Identity: The Jews of Habsburg Austria during World War I* (Oxford University Press, 2004), 82, 98–100. See also David J. Fine, *Jewish Integration in the German Army in the First World War* (De Gruyter, 2012).

through the nineteenth and early twentieth centuries, special care was given to include the imams and their obligations in the reforms.[138] Reforms in 1913 saw imams assigned down to the battalion level (roughly 800 men), who in turn were supervised by a regimental imam. Like the German and Austrian examples, a precise accounting of the total number of imams in service is elusive. In most ways Ottoman imams were engaged in the same religious and morale-inspiring duties as their Christian chaplain counterparts. They led the call to prayer, provided religious instruction and personal counseling, and assisted officers in maintaining order and discipline. This latter role was especially necessary given the high rate of desertion in the Ottoman Army. Imams were regularly engaged as intermediaries to help convince deserters to return to their units. They were also charged with delivering special sermons as the circumstance warranted emphasizing the martial nature of their Islamic faith, going to the point of warning that shirking and desertion were a sin. The personal courage and fighting ability of imams were also regularly tested. They were regularly ordered to take part in attacks alongside the men in their battalion, their own readiness to fight the enemy an example to the more reluctant soldiers.[139]

European officers commanding the African and Indian troops were acutely aware of the religious needs of their soldiers. Individual faith-based dietary restrictions were observed, especially in training camps and hospitals. These extended not only to who was permitted to handle food in the kitchens, but to how meat was butchered and stored, and to maintaining supplies of special food items in hospitals. Religious texts and chaplains appropriate to each faith were provided. Special care was taken to allow soldiers the opportunity to observe their specific festivals and periods of fast: Ramadan and Eid for Muslims, Baisakhi for Sikhs, Diwali for Hindus.

---

[138] Mehmet Beşikçi, "Domestic Aspects of Ottoman Jihad: The Role of Religious Motifs and Religious Agents in the Mobilization of the Ottoman Army," in Erik-Jan Zürcher, *Jihad and Islam in World War I: Studies on the Ottoman Jihad on the Centenary of Snouck Hurgronje's 'Holy War Made in Germany'* (Leiden University Press, 2016), 95–134, here 104.

[139] *Ibid.*, 104–105.

Where possible, allowances were made for the burial and preparation of the dead. Special crematoria were operated to attend to the remains of Hindu and Sikh soldiers, whereas Muslims were buried in services led by imams.[140]

In all cases, chaplains were expected to model the highest moral and patriotic values for their men. Their presence was the fulfillment of an arrangement between the religious and the secular states that can be dated back to the last century of the Roman Empire, if not even before. If the church hierarchies sanctioned war as just and necessary, then by extension they were participants in the conflict. Chaplains were present not only to fulfill the spiritual needs of the soldiers and to attend to the orderly transmission of their immortal souls to the afterlife. They were expected to demonstrate the filial loyalty obligation of every man in uniform to their government and monarch. This was more difficult perhaps in the case of the republics in wartime; but at least in the American case, the president could be seen as the agent of a divine mandate accomplished through popular election. Chaplains were also invested with the trust of the nation to protect their young men from the earthly temptations that so often followed armies from encampment to the zone of combat.

The duties of chaplains were for the most part similar across the armies. Their primary obligations were to maintain the morale of the rank and file through their conduct and active ministrations through the ceremonial practices and sacraments of their faith. Allowances were made for the physical conditions of the front. Where practicable battalion and regimental services would be held in the appropriate public buildings or open space. When permitted by their military commanders, chaplains could also conduct civilian services for local folk. Such gatherings provided windows for French and Belgian civilians into the lives and motivations of their English-speaking allies. The results were generally mixed, with the two sides looking at each other with bemusement at their own religious customs.[141]

---

[140] Kant, "If I Die Here," 115.
[141] Stephen Bellis, *Faith of Our Fathers: Catholic Chaplains with the British Army on the Western Front 1916–19* (Helion & Company Limited, 2018), 47–48; Patrick Carey, "The First World War and Catholics in the United States," in

Pastoral activities included the mundane acts of support for the living and coordinating the passing of the deceased. In line units, chaplains offered personal spiritual and collegial counseling to enlisted men and officers alike. The better ones shared in the personal triumphs and failings their men experienced in the field and through letters from home. Others might offer their services to write letters for the illiterate soldiers to send back to their families or take care to purchase special treats for the men closest to them while on leave or temporary posting away from the regiment. In multidenominational armies (particularly the British and American forces), there was pressure to use these encounters to win converts through their example, an act much rarer than popular literary accounts might suggest. One report identifies only four thousand converts to Catholicism occurring in the entire British Army over the course of the war.[142]

Chaplains assigned to hospitals were kept busy assisting medical orderlies and nurses treating wounded soldiers. Unlike physicians and nurses, chaplains continued to interact with the wounded after their initial treatment. In addition to the public display of prayer – itself important for morale among the wounded and the medical services cadre – they paid regular visits to recovering soldiers to read letters, books, and poems, or to help them write letters home. Chaplains were also admonished to acquire and maintain their own cache of first aid supplies, to either give directly to the first aid medicos working in the field or to use themselves to ease the pain and suffering of those wounded in the field.[143]

A grim obligation was to assist in preparing the dead for their interment or transfer home. Chaplains engaged in rituals of preparing the dead in hospitals for funeral; washing the bodies, preparing the privileged few for return home; and carefully reviewing their belongings for potentially incriminating or embarrassing postcards, prophylactics, or letters from illicit partners. In the trenches, such preparations were often rushed, and

Gordon L. Heath, ed., *American Churches and the First World War* (Pickwick Publications, 2016), 32–52, here 46.

[142] Bellis, *Faith of Our Fathers*, 49.

[143] *Ibid*., 48–49; Albert I. Slomovitz, *The Fighting Rabbis: Jewish Military Chaplains and American History* (NYU Press, 1998), 50–51.

consisted of a quick search of uniforms and kit bags. After collecting the last effects of the dead, chaplains wrote letters to the surviving family, often affirming the deceased had lived a clean and moral life and was assured of salvation. Such duties were time-consuming, not to mention potentially demoralizing for the chaplain himself, but they were also an essential activity in a mass industrial war. The greater the reliance on citizens to potentially sacrifice their lives for the state, the more critical the need to display proper deference to the surviving family. At the very least the illusion of meaningful death had to be maintained. Any failure to provide meaningful closure could potentially disrupt the entire war effort. Russia's leaving the war in 1917, and the disintegration of support for the war among the Central Powers in 1918, can be tied in part to just this type of moral collapse. If maintaining domestic morale was a critical theater of operations, then chaplains occupied an essential, if not strategic, role in this area.

The military institutions on both sides of the wire had additional, secularized roles for chaplains that could interrupt their devotional and pastoral activities. Chaplains were expected to be present at the delivery of capital sentences following courts-martial, both to offer some hope of salvation for the convicted soldier and to preside over last rites following execution. They were also expected to assist officers in censoring mail, acting here again as part of a coercive-oriented system of total control. Chaplains were often charged with organizing entertainments for soldiers outside of the line and were expected to assist with imposing discipline and order if need be. If conditions warranted, they were also expected to serve as tutors or instructors for illiterate enlisted men, helping them learn to read and write.[144]

Ultimately the chaplain's duties, religious and secular, centered around making sense of the war for the enlisted soldiers. On both sides, they were given regular dispatches, reports, and sermons for distribution to their congregations. The worst of these reports were essentially propaganda, dismissed out of hand by soldiers. The message varied. Russian Orthodox literature sent to the front promoted the war within the context of a holy obligation, one which would see the reclamation of Constantinople by the

---

[144] Bellis, *Faith of Our Fathers*, 49–50.

forces of Eastern Christianity. In the German and Austro-Hungarian armies, efforts to share the official news of the war's progress collided head on with the realities of 1916 and 1917. In the West, German forces were just barely hanging on in the aftermath of Verdun and the Somme, while on the Eastern Front, German successes were offset by the near collapse of the *k.u.k.* army. The Italian Catholic hierarchy saw this as an opportunity to reunite "real" Italy (spiritual, religious culture) with "legal" Italy (the secular state), and in so doing provide a platform for reinvigorating the nation.[145]

A controversial practice was the role of chaplains and civilian religious leaders in blessing the weapons of war. The practice represents a critical dividing line between what is necessary for raising morale and maintaining the public spirit in wartime and that which is in turn an immoral call for divine sanction in killing. The outcry against the blessing of weapons was swift. In Austria-Hungary, Catholic priests argued the act was done only at the request of the state, and that it was never intended as a sanction of the war, but rather to call upon God to help bring about a swift end to the war by showing his favor for their own through the blessing. Reasoning that it was God, not the priest, who was actually blessing the weapon, and that the guns and artillery pieces were tools, nothing more, the Church attempted to thread the theological and moral needle to escape blame for its part in extending the conflict.[146]

The issues of critical supply shortages and the constant need for emotional and moral support fostered a general sense of ecumenical tolerance and cooperation that would last after the war and help ease the passage to a more humanistic outlook among the mainstream denominations. In both the British and French armies, Protestant chaplains and rabbis took on the role of confessor for dying and wounded Catholic soldiers. Catholic priests, on the other hand, found they were equally capable of delivering sermons to Protestants and leading prayers at the Passover Seder.[147] In the American Expeditionary Force, the shortage of chaplains and the sheer number of

---

[145] Senin, "Russian Army Chaplains", 47, Houlihan, *Catholicism and the Great War*, 104–105; Gooch, *The Italian Army and the First World War*, 164.

[146] Houlihan, *Catholicism and the Great War*, 55.

[147] Becker, *War and Faith*, 43.

religious denominations and confessions within the army meant that all faiths were to be treated with respect. Chaplains were expected to be prepared to attend to the needs of all soldiers; uniformed rabbis, priests, and ministers shared their liturgies and rituals to attend to the living and the dying alike.[148] In the German Army, similar efforts at ecumenical cooperation were for the most part equally successful. The one blind spot was in the incorporation of rabbis into the ranks of military chaplains. Thirty rabbis were retained by the War Ministry as unpaid volunteers until 1915. Anti-Semitism remained prevalent among Christian officers and enlisted men alike. Even other chaplains persisted in their prejudice against their Jewish compatriots.[149] Ecumenicalism clearly had its limits.

For their own part, the common soldier had two general opinions about the chaplains they encountered. Those who remained aloof and distant from their assigned flock, who mingled only with officers, and who could be relied upon to show up first in the chow line and last when it came time for pastoral call in the trenches, were treated with a blend of skeptical disdain and outright ridicule by the private soldier.[150] Those who took the time to learn the names of their charges, who helped illiterate men write short letters home, who showed enough care for their men's welfare through personal sacrifice, but who also turned a blind eye (or ear) to their less venal (though perhaps obscene) actions, won the men's respect. Perhaps not surprisingly, Catholic chaplains were admired more than their Protestant counterparts in the English and German armies. The immediate need to provide extreme unction for dead and dying soldiers of the faith placed Catholic chaplains more directly in harm's way, which was perceived by infantrymen as a desire to share in their suffering, rather than hide away behind the lines. No less important – at least in the British case – were the class origins of the respective clergy. Anglican, Presbyterian, and Methodist clergymen were largely products of the educated middle class. Catholic chaplains, particularly Irish Catholics, were more likely to come from the

---

[148] Faulkner, *Pershing's Crusaders*, 422.

[149] Tim Grady, *A Deadly Legacy: German Jews and the Great War* (Yale University Press, 2017), 72–73; Slomovitz, *The Fighting Rabbis*, 58.

[150] Wilkinson, *The Church of England*, 110–122.

working class, and thus shared outlooks and customs with their enlisted congregations. Not all Protestant clergy shunned front line service; indeed, those who did share the experience of combat with the fighting men found their trust reciprocated many times. But the perception that Catholic chaplains were somehow more courageous or selfless than their Protestant compatriots survived the war.[151]

Dissent and Resistance

Just as the First World War introduced new concepts of total war and mobilization, it also saw the rise of new categories of pacifist dissent and state coercion. Wartime necessity, and the encroaching existential character of the conflict, created a growing sense of urgency on the part of the state to take full control of its resources – including its citizens – to achieve total victory. Such rationale provides insight into the relationships forged between organized religion and the state during the war. However, the tradition of Christian pacifism was also strong, and presented no shortage of midnight dilemmas for believers. Clearly the majority of conscripts and volunteers reconciled their Christian belief with the state imperative for war. To a large part this was the mandate of just war theologians, crafting a case for mortal violence as a legitimate Christian act under specific conditions. But internalized narratives about personal identity also played a role; as noted earlier, citizenship was negotiated between secular statist obligations and religious moral sensibilities. For far too many people, compliance with the demands of the wartime state was extended freely, with little or no self-recrimination.

But what of those who rejected the legalistic and moralistic case for participating in war? As millions of men were called to arms across the world, their act of civic responsibility was countered in dramatic public fashion by individuals expressing moral rejection of war and violence. Thousands of men risked imprisonment and social pariah status to stand aside from the war on religious grounds. Castigated and jailed, threatened with callous mistreatment, torture, and death threats, the conscientious

---

[151] *Ibid.*, 118–119, 132–135; Faulkner, *Pershing's Crusaders*, 424–428; Schweitzer, *The Cross and the Trenches*, 169–171.

objector has become, at least for historians, a symbol of the futility of hope in the face of mass war hysteria, if not a forlorn role model for future generations of pacifists.

In Britain, the First World War provided a unique test case for aspiring pacifists. The Conscription Act of January 1916 not only introduced the concept of universal military service in Britain, it also created the concept of conscientious objector.[152] Three categories were acknowledged in the Conscription Act: those who could serve in the military in a noncombatant capacity, those who would not serve in the military, but would agree to civilian war work, and finally those who rejected any work that could be seen as supporting the war effort in any way. An estimated 16,500 men reported as objectors. The overwhelming majority – some 15,000 – were classified as either military noncombatants (3,300 men) or civilian war workers (11,700 in total). The remaining 1,500 were labeled "absolutists." Contrary to expectations, there is no clear way to identify the objectors on the basis of religious affiliation or sentiment. Certainly the nonconformist denominations – Quakers, Christadelphians, Jehovah's Witnesses, and Plymouth Brethren – stand out. Of the mainstream denominations, the Methodists appear to have been the largest group. Anglicans only made up 7 percent of the group – lower, Alan Wilkinson notes, than the atheists (12 percent).[153]

Conscientious objectors were subject to the full coercive and punitive weight of the British state at war. At the very least, they were harangued in the most vile language publicly, accused not only of cowardice, but perverse disregard for the safety of their own families and the sanctity of their homes. Numerous conscription tribunals exacerbated the situation by refusing to accept conscientious objection as legitimate grounds for exempting men from service, ordering them to report for duty despite the conditions of the Conscription Act. Ultimately some 6,000 men were imprisoned for rejecting the tribunal's verdict or for ignoring the process altogether. A handful were sentenced to death, though their sentences were commuted by Field Marshall Douglas Haig. In 1917, custody of imprisoned conscientious objectors who refused to accommodate to the conditions of the

---

[152] Wilkinson, *The Church of England*, 46.

[153] *Ibid.*, 47.

Conscription Act were transferred to the Home Office, which established a work camp in Dartmoor. Conditions here were austere, contributing to the death of several inmates.[154]

American dissenters faced similar treatment. The Wilson Administration's heavy hand came as a surprise to many, given his support for neutrality before April 1917. In short order, his government turned its full legal and extralegal powers against those conscientious objectors who pursued the same measured neutrality he advocated two years before. Chief among the reasons for this change is his own religious sentiment and conviction. More than any of his political contemporaries, Woodrow Wilson viewed his role as president through a faith-based lens. The scion of a long line of Presbyterian elders, religion was central to his moral and intellectual development throughout his life. As a strict Calvinist doctrinaire, Wilson believed that God was the absolute sovereign over the world and its people, and that he was the instrument of His will. In his professional life before entering politics, Wilson pursued the study of history and political science as much to understand the hand of the divine in human affairs as to chart the course of parliamentary systems.[155]

Wilson's faith could be obdurate; he believed his relationship with God gave him insights into the morality of governance that other leaders – domestic and global – lacked. Before 1917, this justified repeated intervention in the Caribbean, all efforts determined to impose his "better judgment" on recalcitrant neighbors. The war in Europe was a different matter entirely, but this did not preclude his acting upon his religious impulse for peace. In the first two years of the war, Wilson advocated arbitration, offering to serve as a neutral mediator between the two sides. Only after his advances were rebuffed, and German actions (real and alleged) revealed an assumed diabolic edge, did Wilson begin to turn toward the Allied cause. 1917 and the resumption of unrestricted submarine warfare, and the failed

[154] *Ibid.,* 48–49.

[155] Gary Scott Smith, *Faith and the Presidency: From George Washington to George W. Bush* (Oxford University Press, 2006), 161, 165, 171; Malcolm D. Magee, *What the World Should Be: Woodrow Wilson and the Crafting of a Faith-Based Foreign Policy* (Baylor University Press, 2008), 65.

German effort to enlist Mexico as a counterweight to America in the event of war, saw Wilson change his mind. Yet even here, historians note, Wilson cast himself as a Christ-like figure, the decision to go to war his personal Gethsemane. Agonizing over the prospect of war after so many years of championing peace, Wilson ultimately turned to scripture and history to square his decision. Casting the decision in his address to Congress asking for a declaration of war as a moral obligation to rescue the world – even the German people – from the jackboot of Prussian militarism, he ultimately invoked God's blessing[156]

Once set on the course of war against Germany, Wilson transferred his moral conviction toward the objective of victory in the name of God and His will. As Gary Scott Smith notes, calls to "make the world safe for democracy" and to "end all wars" were as much religious statements as they were progressive appeals. "In the ensuing months, many Christian clergy used pulpit and print to strongly support this 'war of righteousness.' . . . Wilson fostered this image of the United States as a righteous, redemptive agent, calling the nation 'an instrument in the hands of God' to secure liberty for humanity."[157] Those who resisted his appeals – former pacifist political allies, communities of religious conviction, radical progressive reformers – were now cast as misinformed and self-serving obstructionists, their convictions turned into evidence of unwitting compliance with the enemy of civilization itself. Perversely their ensuing persecution by the government reflected of the power of their message in a wartime society that had once accepted it as the political norm. As Kathleen Kennedy points out, what ensued was more than the reversal of the progressive agenda championed by the peacetime President Wilson; it was a contest between two different faiths of freedom.[158] The difference, however, is that where she

---

[156] Smith, *Faith and the Presidency*, 176–178; Magee, *What the World Should Be*, 76; "An Address to a Joint Session of Congress," (April 2, 1917), in Arthur S. Link, *The Papers of Woodrow Wilson*, Volume 41: January 24–April 6, 1917 (Princeton University Press, 1983), 519–527.

[157] Smith, *Faith and the Presidency*, 180.

[158] Kathleen Kennedy, "Civil Liberties," in Ross A. Kennedy, ed., *A Companion to Woodrow Wilson* (Wiley-Blackwell, 2013), 323–342, here 340.

speaks of faith in the metaphorical sense, of being part of a larger challenge between the proponents of limitless federal power and the advocates of civil liberties, the fight was actually rooted in a religious argument. If Wilson and his government were claiming a prerogative to act in the name of divine will, then resistance to their efforts, no matter how well-intentioned, were misinformed acts of defiance.

The Selective Service Act of 1917 granted exemptions on religious grounds for those who were part of an established recognized church that forbade military service as it contributed to killing. During the First World War, some 64,000 men claimed conscientious objector status. Some 43,000 men were granted an exemption, leaving over 21,000 to be inducted. The majority of these dissenters agreed to serve in whatever capacity the army deemed fit for them. Another 1,300 men agreed to serve in a noncombatant capacity, while 1,200 were furloughed for the duration of the war. Ultimately 940 men were confined in training camps alongside recruits undergoing basic training, and 504 were court-martialed. Just as in the United Kingdom, there was no clear means to classify them by denomination. The older dissenter churches – Quakers, Mennonites, Anabaptists – were nearly united in their objection to the war. They were joined by numerous small Pentecostal churches, particularly in the Appalachian South. Otherwise, however, no major Protestant denomination staked out an anti-war position after April 1917. And as for Catholics, the American cardinals and bishops alike pushed back against Pope Benedict XV's call to pacifism, arguing instead for remaining loyal to the state.[159]

American dissenters faced a wide range of sanctions, ranging from public shaming and ridicule to imprisonment under harsh conditions without trial. As mentioned, for 504 men, their religious obligation and acts of conscience led them to military justice, court-martialed as draft evaders and deserters. In many cases, the harsh treatment of religious objectors stemmed from the collective anxiety and outrage of the local or state communities at the prospect of individuals winning an exemption from service denied to their own menfolk. The treatment of four Hutterite farmers from South

---

[159] Duane C. S. Stoltzfus, *Pacifists in Chains: The Persecution of Hutterites During the Great War* (Johns Hopkins University Press, 2013), 206–207.

Dakota, sentenced to twenty years hard labor at Alcatraz Island in July 1918, is one example of note. The four men were confined in the absolute darkness of the island's cellars, dangling from the ceiling in irons, on bread and water rations, wearing only their underwear. Charged by their home state under the terms of the Espionage Act of 1917, the moral conscience of the Hutterite dissenters was transformed into a willful act of treasonable defiance by members of a German-speaking community living as aliens in the midst of the English-speaking majority.[160] Other dissenters faced equally harsh treatment from the state and citizens alike. Mocked and humiliated in public, dissenters who were ordered to report to military camps were liable to be physically attacked by other soldiers. Many received ad hoc field discipline that was reminiscent of the nineteenth century, such as being tied to a post or sent alone to an outpost under heavy fire. If this failed to produce results, the objector was placed in formal custody as a deserter. Once remanded to the stockade, they were often sentenced to hard labor, supplemented by beatings and imposed deprivations by the guards. The entire regimen was intended to humiliate and cajole conscientious objectors into accepting military service, no matter the cost to their individual rights and liberties.[161]

Unlike her opponents, Germany did not officially accommodate the prospect of military exemption on the grounds of conscientious objection. Cross-cultural persecution, censorship, and incarceration were held up as the wages of active pacifism for German conscientious objectors. Extreme cases – generally those who persisted despite the pressure of the state – faced medicalized persecution. Labeled insane by the state, they were incarcerated in mental hospitals, where they were subjected to the full range of therapeutic treatment. The examples of Karl Liebknecht and Ernst Friedrich, both socialist opponents of the war imprisoned for their

---

[160] *Ibid.*, 104–137.

[161] Anne-Marie Pennington, "Struggling Not to Fight: The Experience of Radicals and Pacifists during World War I," in Timothy C. Dowling, ed., *Personal Perspectives: World War I* (ABC-CLIO, Inc., 2006), 297–322, here 306–308; Gerlof D. Homan, *American Mennonites and the Great War, 1914–1918* (Herald Press, 1994), 103.

activism, are most frequently cited as evidence of the fate awaiting citizens of conscience. While the full coercive weight of the state was levied against political objectors, however, those who resisted participation on religious grounds were generally accommodated. The regime continued to observe an earlier accommodation with Mennonites granting them conditional exemption from combat service. Members of other smaller Protestant sects – Seventh Day Adventists and Jehovah's Witnesses, for example – were likewise either placed in noncombatant positions or quietly dismissed from service altogether. So long as the religious objectors were quiet about their status and did not take part in any public activism against the war, the government was willing to leave them be.[162]

Conclusion

Even after a century, understanding how soldiers participating in the First World War remained motivated and kept up their morale is a complex matter. The tremendous stresses of combat and daily survival quickly wore men down. Moments of despair turned into disillusionment, which could quickly turn to mutiny, revolution, and defeat. The challenge for historians is how best to assess the balance between assent and despondency by soldiers. Historian André Loez summarizes the challenges researchers face:

> [M]ethodological difficulties in interpreting primary sources (some letters or diaries will show evidence of the acceptance of the war yet their author may desert, conversely, some soldiers who write of their refusal or disapproval of the conflict can nonetheless show great resolve and a willingness to fight) indicate that the question of soldiers' attitudes

---

[162] Ingrid Sharp, "Life was even tougher for the German conscientious objectors of World War I," *The Conversation*, May 15, 2014. http://theconversation.com/life-was-even-tougher-for-the-german-conscientious-objectors-of-world-war-i-26715 Accessed November 9, 2019; Guido Grünewald, "German Resistance to World War One," Peace History Conference 2016, October 14, 2016. Leeds, UK. www.abolishwar.org.uk/uploads/1/6/6/2/16622106/german_resistance_to_world_war_one_-_english_version.pdf Accessed November 9, 2016.

towards war needs to be framed carefully, to be put in context, always taking into account the variety of military situations and of belligerent nations.[163]

Loez identifies four specific factors that defined the limits of soldiers' endurance in the First World War: "military configuration, political or ideological affiliation, rank and class, and national integration."[164] Absent from his formulation is the subject of this section – faith. Efforts to identify the moral and emotional limits of the men who waged the war without accounting for the strength and succor they found within their personal beliefs in the divine and its power to intervene or shield them from harm, or the convictions they held of a just afterlife, are incomplete. The various miracles, talismans, and often repeated accounts of supernatural and divine intervention represented tangible evidence of the power of faith. It is easy to dismiss these all as superstition; doing so obscures the fact that for men confronting the prospect of death and mutilation every day, the artifacts and rituals provided some intangible, yet for the individual, real emotional shelter from the crushing stress of war. Religious faith bolstered the courage of men in extreme situations, while providing further strength in the communal observance of ritual with fellow believers. Chaplains were a tangible bridge between the normalcy of peacetime life, the current state of conflict, and the promise of redemption. Not all realized their potential, but their presence in even the most anticlerical national armies helped sustain the discipline of soldiers and their compliance with the war effort far more effectively than more coercive means.

The question of dissent and the harsh measures imposed upon conscientious objectors is one of conflicting definitions of faith. Religious dissenters asserted that a higher morality dictated their resistance. The state in turn claimed its mandate to wage war was just and opposition on moral grounds was misinformed, and must be dealt with harshly, lest such beliefs spread.

---

[163] André Loez, "Between Acceptance and Refusal – Soldiers' Attitudes Towards War," *1914–1918 Online: International Encyclopedia of the First World War.* https://encyclopedia.1914-1918-online.net/article/between_acceptance_and_refusal_-_soldiers_attitudes_towards_war Accessed June 11, 2020.

[164] *Ibid.*

In the end though, faith was much more than a crutch to sustain troubled and frightened men through a crucible of suffering. It gave soldiers, from fervent believers to casual foxhole converts to committed skeptics, the ability to press on as their friends and comrades fell beside them or were annihilated in a bombardment or suffocated from gas attack. Faith provided hope of a slender chance to survive against odds and to return home. It is difficult to quantify something as personal as faith, but it should be considered as a factor – even a peripheral one – toward the ability of the armies and men to stay in the fight.

3 Grief and Memory

Gradually the guns fell silent. For the most part, soldiers put up their rifles, stepped away from their guns, and returned home to their grateful families. What, though, about the millions of widows and orphans who were left behind? As Richard Schweitzer notes,

> For civilians on the home front, the war was an agonizing waiting experience: waiting for letters from their loved ones at the front, waiting for published accounts of the latest offensive, waiting for the casualty lists to appear in *The Times* or other newspapers, and finally waiting for the letter or telegram to inform them that a loved one was wounded or killed in action.[165]

For them, the end of battle did not necessarily mean that the war was over. Long decades of grieving and fighting civilian political apathy remained. In the immediate aftermath of the war, Western survivors turned to a range of coping strategies to rationalize the loss of their loved ones. Formal organized religious traditions led the way, particularly within Catholic communities. Rituals of mourning and the promise of reunion and reward in the afterlife, not to mention the concept of direct divine intercession through the agency of angels, saints, clergymen, and devout laymen, sustained many

---

[165] Richard Schweitzer, *The Cross and the Trenches: Religious Faith and Doubt among British and American Great War Soldiers* (Praeger Publishers, 2003), 141.

millions of grieving families. Where religion failed to offer solace, many turned toward the prospect of direct interaction with the dead. Spiritualism in its many forms – such as séance, tarot readings, spirit photography – grew exponentially in popularity, reaching a level of acceptance not seen since the American Civil War.[166]

Rituals of grief intersected with the task of preserving the memory of the fallen generation. Battlefields, cemeteries, and commissioned memorials became blank slates upon which competing narratives of the war and its toll were presented, debated, and validated. Among the victorious Allies (and the Associated Power, the United States), the challenge was to ensure the living never forgot or forsook the dead who gave freely of their lives. The narratives pursued by each nation differed in tone and purpose. After 1921, many Italian public memorials evoked the elan and martial spirit of the dead in a virtual cult of the fallen. The purpose here was not to atone for their death, however, but rather to channel the war experience in line with Fascist militaristic ideology. Likewise French efforts tended to elevate the virtues of the secular Third Republic and its new accommodation with Catholicism forged in the trenches. For the defeated Germans, Austrians, and Hungarians, commemoration was grudging and stinging. Through the war, political and cultural elites heralded the magnificence of German/Habsburg culture and the inevitability of victory over their uncouth, materialistic, and cultureless foes. Defeat triggered a long overdue cultural debate over the state's place in daily life, and a rejection of traditional institutions – including the Lutheran establishment in Prussia – that had thrown itself so fully behind the war.[167]

The pursuit of meaning from the war would establish the context for a set of significant challenges to the legitimacy of Judeo-Christian theology in its history. Western elites who participated in the war saw the faith of their youth shattered. Many civilian onlookers and participants in the

---

[166] Drew Gilpin Faust, *This Republic of Suffering: Death and the American Civil War* (Vintage, 2009), 179–186.

[167] Oliver Janz, "Mourning and the Cult of the Fallen (Italy)," *1914–1918 Online: International Encyclopedia of the First World War*. https://encyclopedia.1914-1918-online.net/article/mourning_and_cult_of_the_fallen_italy (Accessed November 30, 2019).

mobilization of society to wage the war became skeptics of moral authority in all forms. When religion proved insufficient, new modes of accounting for untimely death and its aftermath were engaged, to varied effect. Many social historians pursue the adoption of romanticized supernatural modes of grief – spiritualism in particular – as a coping mechanism. No less important, however, were theoretical and applied scientific concepts and processes. And yet, not all abandoned faith, which itself proved to be a remarkably malleable thing. Over the following decade, a lively debate over the inherent morality of pure science – as embodied in Albert Einstein's relativity theory – acquired the moral authenticity of religious dogma for many millions of people disenchanted with the promises of an inconsistent theology.[168] Engaging science in the interwar years was not an automatic progression to atheism or agnosticism, however. More accurately, it reveals how individuals sought to adapt their faith outlooks to accept and account for the depth of their own loss.

Spiritualism and the War

In his ground-breaking work, *Sites of Memory, Sites of Mourning: The Great War in European Cultural History*, Jay Winter introduces readers to the prospect that spiritualism rivaled religious faith among soldiers and their families during the First World War. This mixture of superstition, folkways, trust in cheap tchotchkes, and trench rumors certainly helped soldiers cope with the prospect of death – if not utter physical annihilation. Working-class families, both urban and rural, likewise placed no small amount of trust in these talismans and rituals for preserving their loved ones.[169]

Postmortem spiritualism was a different factor altogether. According to historian David Cannadine, the British spiritualist movement became one of

---

[168] See Matthew Stanley, *Einstein's War: How Relativity Triumphed Amid the Vicious Nationalism of World War I* (Dutton, 2019).

[169] Jay Winter, *Sites of Memory, Sites of Mourning: The Great War in European Cultural History* (Cambridge University Press, 1995), 64–67. See also Owen Davies, *A Supernatural War: Magic, Divination, and Faith during the First World War* (Oxford University Press, 2019), 54–98.

the nation's most widespread cultural phenomena of the First World War. Growing slowly in Britain before the war, attracting a number of noteworthy adherents in the British political and literary establishment, the movement exploded from barely over 150 societies to 309 in 1919; by the mid-1930s, Cannadine cites reports of over 2,000 spiritualist groups in the United Kingdom, with over 250,000 members. For the grieving, spiritualism offered a chance to connect with the dead who had passed over to a better life. In this way, he notes, "If Armistice Day was the *public recognition of bereavement*, the Spiritualist movement, by contrast, was the *private denial of death*."[170] Adherents employed seances, spectral photography, spiritual writing, and other techniques to permit closure for the grieving, even as they were greeted with skepticism and mockery by others. Winter considers that this emphasis on spiritualism represents how the First World War sustained Victorian cultural practices regarding the afterlife. Claims that the war was a tragic, yet critical, rejection of tradition in favor of a new ironic and skeptical modern sensibility are premature. Winter writes:

> Some of these practices and beliefs were superstitious. Others entered the realm of the uncanny, the paranormal, the necromantic or the mystical. All shared a tendency to slide from metaphors about remembering those who have died to the metaphysics of life after death. The 1914–19 conflict certainly did not create these modes of thought, but neither did the war discredit or destroy them. Millions needed all the help they could get. Should we really be surprised that the magical and mystical realm flared up at a time of mass death and destruction?[171]

---

[170] David Cannadine, "War and Death, Grief and Mourning in Modern Britain," in Joachim Whaley, ed., *Mirrors of Mortality: Studies in the Social History of Death* (Routledge, 1981, 2011), Kindle Version. Location 6264, 6320–6321.

[171] Winter, *Sites of Memory, Sites of Mourning*, 76.

In this way, the First World War offers direct comparisons with the American Civil War. Drew Gilpin Faust also considers spiritualism to be a cultural legacy founded in wartime, an attempt by grief-stricken families to obtain some contact with the dead. The immediate trauma of unexpected loss of life disproportionate with early expectations overwhelmed traditional rituals of grief and mourning.[172] The toll in both cases was so great, it affected how the cultures of the United States (in the former) and Western Europe (and again, the United States, in the latter) perceived death and its place in the lives of survivors. Resolving the untimely and dramatic deaths, enough to cut into the promise of an entire generation, would prove to be a nearly insurmountable task. Added to this was the insistence of many families to know the circumstances of the death of their fallen and missing. Being denied the opportunity to oversee the proper interment of their dead family members was one matter – again, the sheer scale of death in battle precluded individual burial, let alone transport home of the bodies. The destructive killing power in both wars was such that a large number of dead could not be properly identified, let alone in some cases even found. A new category of "missing" was added to the casualty rolls; not for tallying those deserters, malingerers, and shirkers who ran off without leave before or during battle, but to account for those presumed dead of whom there was insufficient physical evidence remaining to identify them.

As both Faust and (to a lesser degree) Winter acknowledge, the appeal of spiritualism for many families was reassurance: reassurance that their son, husband, or brother did not suffer unduly, physically or emotionally, at the time of their passing. Faust introduces the Victorian concept of "The Good Death" as a moral construct that became central to the pursuit of closure for grieving families. As much a secular cultural concept as a religious premise, The Good Death ensured that one lived a life rich in meaning and promise prior to their mortal injury. The fallen soldier was assumed to have fought

---

[172] In the American Civil War, an estimated 620,000 (roughly 2 percent of the population), and in the British case during the First World War, approximately 886,000 (about 1.79 percent of the total population). See Faust, *This Republic of Suffering*, xi; www.nationalarchives.gov.uk/help-with-your-research/research-guides/deaths-first-and-second-world-wars/ (Accessed December 9, 2019).

bravely, selflessly, and well, at peace with their lives before dying. They also were expected to have not suffered, their death to have been sudden, without pain, and leaving behind a recognizable corpse that appeared to be sleeping, not displaying terror or shock at being killed.[173] Similar fears and expectations were an underpinning for families during and after the First World War as well. Clairvoyants and mediums offered an assurance that clergymen and priests could not: by directly contacting the dead, they could give testimony that they died well, and were in a better place, which was precisely the balm the grieving family members – the majority women – so desperately wanted.[174] The issue of legitimacy is beyond the point. Grieving families did not consider the prospect of charlatanry and fraud; or at least, they put the idea out of mind for the immediacy of the moment. They were willing to take the leap into the unknown if it gave them understanding of how their own dead sons and husbands met a Good Death.

Other combatant nations – especially France, Germany, Italy, the United States, and the British Dominions – experienced similar revivals in spiritualist rituals and practices after the war. Many noteworthy figures – Èmile Durkheim, Eric Ludendorff, Sir Arthur Conan Doyle – are associated with spiritualist circles during and after the war. Following the contours of British spiritualism over the 1920s, one can certainly infer similar ebbs and flows of personal reliance on spirit mediums elsewhere.

The challenge is the limits of historiography on such an esoteric premise (the intersection of occultism and military history). Annette Becker acknowledges the state of French scholarship in this area is thin.[175] Similar deficiencies appear with regard to German studies of grief and bereavement, where the emphasis is on the establishment of cults of the

---

[173] Faust, *This Republic of Suffering*, 7–10.

[174] Joy Damousi, "Mourning Practices," in Jay Winter, ed., *The Cambridge History of the First World War*. Volume III: Civil Society (Cambridge University Press), 358–384, here 382.

[175] Annette Becker, *War and Faith: The Religious Imagination in France, 1914–1930* (Berg, 1998), 104.

fallen and their relationship to the rise of National Socialism.[176] In the case of Russia, the entire issue of studying grief and the First World War is stymied by the post-Tsarist Bolshevik regime's policy of restricting any official or informal commemoration of the Imperial Russian dead, in preference to emphasizing the fallen heroes of the Revolution.[177] And yet, even though culturally distinct, there remains a universality of grief that transcends linguistic constraints. Historian Joy Damousi aptly summarizes the universality of rituals of loss around the world when she notes:

> Individual mourning was replicated around the world – in all parts of Europe, Australasia, Asia, Africa, and the United States – from wherever and whichever country men were lost. However, mourning had changed in some ways. Communities of mourners gathered as families and relatives sought and found comfort among themselves and among strangers bound by the unique and ghastly circumstances that had befallen them. The outpouring of grief was more acceptable. The search for meaning – both of life and death – more understandable.[178]

Grief Becomes Memory

The scale of death in the First World War, so tremendous and complete in raw numbers, heralded a new age of collective and individual mourning. As we have noted, the resolution of personal grief took many forms. Formal

---

[176] See for example: Silke Fehlemann, "Bereavement and Mourning (Germany)," *1914–1918 Online: International Encyclopedia of the First World War*. https://encyclopedia.1914-1918-online.net/article/bereavement_and_mourning_germany (Accessed December 9, 2019).

[177] Svetlana Iur'evna Malysheva, " Bereavement and Mourning (Russian Empire)," *1914–1918 Online: International Encyclopedia of the First World War*. https://encyclopedia.1914-1918-online.net/article/bereavement_and_mourning_russian_empire (Accessed December 9, 2019).

[178] Damousi, "Mourning Practices," 371.

remembrance was likewise transformed. Part of this was the outcome of the war's scope: there were simply too many dead to allow for traditional rituals of interment. Likewise, so many of the dead would remain missing until long after the moment of their death, their corpses left to decompose in No Man's Land until after the fighting passed them by, that peacetime burial practices were simply impracticable. Many bodies were so shattered by the destructive power they faced there was little left to recognize them. The personal interactions between surviving family and the deceased that marked traditional burials were just not possible for the vast majority of dead. Concerns over public health took precedence over the need for personal closure, as bodies were heaped into mass graves, the only religious niceties observed being the hurried consecration of the dead. Denied the comfort of ritual and collective mourning, families across Europe were genuinely bereft, their unresolved grief creating a sort of living purgatory experience for the parents, spouses, and children left behind.

Grief therefore informed and prompted governments over the next twenty years to frame the war and its grim toll through a series of formal acts of remembrance. The interwar period (1919–1939) is generally presented as an interruption in the larger conflict between Germany and her foes. While the temptation to view the 1920s and 1930s as a sort of breathing space between the two wars is ever present, it is important to note that the decades were also marked by a dramatic cycle of grieving that was still unresolved at the start of the Second World War. In Britain and France, the public affirmation of the dead began with mass displays of commemoration. The November 11, 1920 unveiling of the Cenotaph in London, and the state funeral of the Unknown Soldier in Paris, was the start of the official public commemoration of the war dead. The object of the mass participatory commemoration was to affirm the depth of sacrifice and loss felt by the entire nation. Half gratitude, half mourning, the act quickly acquired several forms. In France, Great Britain, and the United States, the moment of the Western Front Armistice became the core of a national day of thanksgiving. Parades and public addresses presided over (at least until they passed away) by veterans of the war were ritualized acts of public commemoration. Other activities – the sale of paper poppies in the UK and United States, the two minute moment of silence at the time of the armistice – while deliberately constructed, were also cultural artifacts of the war that outlasted the popular memory of events that had long ago crossed from memory into history.[179]

Closely associated with mass commemoration are the many public memorials erected to the memory of the war's dead. While Jay Winter is correct in noting that "[w]ar memorials are collective symbols," for communities united in their grief, they may also be acutely specific and personal.[180] Certainly the larger memorials at or near the battlefields – the Thiepval Arch located at the Somme, or the Douaumont Ossuary at Verdun – act as catalysts for the grieving of national communities. But local communities at home also sought to publicly acknowledge in perpetuity the losses sustained in the war. Throughout Western Europe, small towns and cities alike erected memorials to the local dead. No visit to the British, French, or German countryside is complete without seeing the crosses, statues, and plaques that form the centerpiece of public grief even a century after the war's end. American commemoration was much smaller in scale, but in areas where conscription was particularly strong, bronze and stone doughboys stood vigil over the names of the local dead.[181]

Through the interwar years the process of commemorating the dead became ritualized through various public demonstrations of grief and loss, which over time acquired the legitimacy of tradition. Annual observances of the Armistice, including parades, the presentation of military honors and memorial wreaths before the tombs of the unknowns in the United States and Europe, and the public recitation of the names on community rolls of the dead, became annual events. Family members and former comrades returned to the gravesites of the fallen in France and Belgium, their visits taking on the same character of devotion as the pilgrimages of the faithful to roadside Catholic shrines. Cemetery visits were frequently paired with battlefield tours, creating a more complete circuit of grief and remembrance. Here bereft family members could gain a greater sense of connection with

[179] Fletcher, *Life, Death and Growing Up*, 253.

[180] Winter, *Sites of Memory*, 51; Alan Wilkinson, *The Church of England and the First World War* (The Lutterworth Press, 1978, 1996, 2014), 295–296.

[181] Damousi, "Mourning Practices," 371–372.

their loss, imagining themselves walking the pathways of their dead loved ones, much the same way as pilgrims to Jerusalem could retrace Christ's final days. Battlefield pilgrimages also offered the possibility of closure through personal interaction with veterans on both sides of the line. Widows, mothers, and children could and did engage other mourners and returning veterans in their visits. Encounters with British, French, or more rarely, American visitors allowed grieving families the solace of recognizing their own loss as part of a larger sacrifice. Those who engaged German visitors rediscovered the humanity that all families shared, if they were willing to forgive.

Over time the battlefield and soldiers' cemeteries became a focal point for commemoration unique unto themselves and independent from the domestic sites and rituals of grieving. As the visible scars of the Western Front faded, debates were initiated on both sides of the Atlantic of how to preserve the memory of the war at the knife's point of contact with the enemy. Veterans committees and formal battlefield commissions set out to create a landscape of memorials and markers all along the front. The monuments served two purposes: they fixed in physical space the historical memory of the war for future generations; and they provided another point of contact between the living and the dead. The Anglophone participants took special care to ensure they were well-represented in this space, with the consent of the French and Belgian people. Over the 1920s and 1930s, massive stone memorials were built at the particular sites of interest: the Menin Gate and the Thiepval Arch for the British and Commonwealth armies; the massive Vimy Ridge memorial for Canada; and the tower astride the top of Montfaucon for the American Expeditionary Forces, for example. Built on land forever donated by their host nations, these memorials became and remain the epicenter for ritualized ceremonies of remembrance and continue to occupy a critical place in the itineraries of visitors.

Such large memorials and ossuaries were not the exclusive premise of the state, even those erected by the French Republic. Placed at the sites of the most significant and symbolic battles (from the Allied and American perspectives), the memorials transformed the surrounding landscape into a sacred space. The commemoration of the dead at these locations signaled to the living that their deaths were not in vain, and indeed fulfilled God's plan. Once mere dead soldiers, they were transformed into martyrs for the nation and the divine. As noted, even French memorials adopted this language of reconciliation and faith, taking special care to adopt both the message of the *Union sacrée* and an all-inclusive ecumenism. The ambitions and hopes of the French Catholic bishops were realized – the war did restore the Church to its place in French society. Perhaps not to the desire expected or anticipated, but anticlericalism did recede. No longer seen as a dire threat to the secular Republic, Catholicism was accepted as one aspect of a multifaceted Frenchness. Likewise, postwar Catholicism embraced a new toleration of other faiths – Protestantism, Judaism, Islam – as a result of the war. The ossuaries at Douaumont and Hartmanwillerkopf bear witness to this ecumenism; not only are the remains of all four faiths interred and acknowledged together (along with atheists and free thinkers, incidentally), they also extend the blessing of the Catholic sacrament to all interred within.[182]

The intersection of mourning and faith is not confined to the larger state-sponsored memorials scattered along the Western Front. Smaller memorials placed along the battlefield serve as focal points for local communities' observances, as well as being guide markers for tourists and family members seeking clarity and meaning to the war. Cemeteries were also intended to provide essential way stations for deeply personal observations on faith and grief. While frequently segregated by nationality, graveyards became a common ground for shared reflections between visiting pilgrims from both sides of the war. A shared lingua franca of martyrdom was incorporated into the framing of the dead for the living. As Jonathan Ebel notes, the First World War cemetery exists "as both sacred texts and sacred spaces."[183] The choice of inscriptions, deliberately selected by each nation to convey the uniformity of the classless dead while also noting where possible their unique identities, serve as a virtual hagiography for the fallen. The nearly identical markers, arrayed in symmetrically defined rows, evoke

---

[182] Anthony Fletcher, *Life, Death and Growing Up on the Western Front* (Yale University Press, 2013), 256–258; Becker, *War and Faith*, 125–129.

[183] Jonathan Ebel, *G.I. Messiahs: Soldiering, War, and American Civil Religion* (Yale University Press, 2015), 72.

a wordless sermon on humility before God, the fragility of the flesh, and the endurance of the spirit. Not uncommonly guarded over by stone sentinels, or the flag of the nation, the sacrifice is evoked through public declarations of faith and grief.[184]

Another venue for commemoration were local parish churches. All across Europe, organized religions maintained their own rituals of observance and grief. Catholics, Jews, and Protestants all maintained their own honor rolls of the dead in their congregations. Ruined French and Belgian churches required expensive and time-consuming reconstruction, more often than not with donations from American and English Catholics and well-meaning philanthropists. Away from the front, local churches across Europe and America dedicated pews, wall markers, and stained glass windows to the war dead. Motifs vary – images of Christ, Mary, or angels blessing uniformed men, standing or fallen; trench scenes and parade ground portrayals – but the intention is the same. Windows of Remembrance provide stirring reminders to the family and congregation of the sacrifices made for them and the nation alike.[185]

Yet these efforts to commemorate and honor the fallen lent their discursive weight to postwar revanchism in conservative circles across Europe. Writing for the online encyclopedia of the First World War maintained by the Free University of Berlin and the Bavarian State Library, Oliver Janz observes the intersection between grief and action in some circles:

> There were hardly any consequences of the Great War that were as lasting as the mourning for the dead. In the aftermath of the conflict, one of the main challenges that nations faced was how to cope with the deaths of millions of mostly young men. There was a close affinity between mourning and aggression. The intertwinement of mass death and mass mourning had a destabilizing potential that could only be defused by the political alchemy of patriotic death cults.

[184] *Ibid.*, 74, 83.
[185] Becker, *War and Faith* 155–158.

> These cults of mourning were intended to transform anger
> into awe, sadness into pride, and trauma into consensus.[186]

In the 1920s, Italian Fascists constructed a culture of martyrdom intended superficially to claim that the nation's 700,000 dead were betrayed by the Liberal parliamentarians' failure to secure Italy's war aims. Once secure in power, the Fascist movement continued to exploit this constructed ideology of the nation's dead as a guarantor of national martial political culture and the foundation of their own claims to legitimacy. As the totalitarian impulse gained momentum following the onset of the Great Depression in Europe, the collective grief of the immediate postwar period was appropriated by like-minded National Socialists in Germany, the National Will Party in Hungary, the British Union of Fascists, and others, effectively subverting their message of an international community united in their loss in favor of a more overtly singular purpose rooted in violence and coercion.[187]

Did Religion Fail? The Resilience of Faith during the First World War

The question remains: Did the First World War provide a boost to religious institutions and faith? Scholars routinely identify the war as being secular in context, one in which the values of tradition and religious sentiment were overturned by the rationalism of science and romanticized nationalism. Scholars like Karen Armstrong note how the First World War unleashed powerful conflicting emotions on the world:

> This secular war for the nation had given some of the
> participants experiences associated with the religious

---

[186] Oliver Janz, "Mourning and Cult of the Fallen (Italy), in *1914–1918 Online: International Encyclopedia of the First World War*. https://encyclopedia.1914 -1918-online.net/article/mourning_and_cult_of_the_fallen_italy   (Accessed June 6, 2020).

[187] See Stein Ugelvik Larsen, Bernt Hagtvet, and Jan Peter Myklebust, *Who Were the Fascists? Social Roots of European Fascism* (Universitetsforlaget, 1980), for more detail on individual fascist movements in the interwar period.

traditions: an *ekstatis*, a sense of liberation, freedom, equa-
nimity, community, and a profound relationship with other
human beings, even the enemy. Yet the First World War
heralded a century of unprecedented slaughter and genocide
that was inspired not by religion as people had come to
know it but by an equally commending notion of the sacred:
men fought for power, glory, scarce resources, and above
all, their nation.[188]

And yet, the war is also seen as a watershed moment for fundamentalist
critiques of religion and humanity. The war's violence triggered a dramatic
reassessment of faith throughout the world, leading many to reject the social
modernism that had permeated Christianity, Judaism, and Islam over
previous decades. The contradictions are striking. As the First World
War undermined the faith of millions of persons all across the world, it
also affirmed the literal power of scripture and prophecy for a significant
number as well. At the moment when rationalism and scientific inquiry were
challenging the primacy of God in private and public life, fundamentalist
doctrines were winning disenchanted hearts and minds by preaching a stark,
but basic, message: the Great Adversary, awash in the blood of innocents
cast to the charnel house of war, was ascendant. The End Times were nigh,
and it was time for all men to make ready. Again Armstrong notes the
eschatological message was but one part of a great malaise that had gripped
survivors of the war. "The American fundamentalists' chilling scenario of
the end time, with its wars, bloodshed, and slaughter, is symptomatic of
a deep-rooted distress that cannot be assuaged by cool rational analysis. In
less stable countries, it would be all too easy for a similar malaise, despair,
and fear to erupt in physical violence."[189] One may consider the outbreaks
of mob violence targeting socialists, African Americans, and other ethnic
and religious minorities in the United States during the "Red Summer" of
1919 and after in this context. Violent nativist organizations like the Ku

---

[188] Karen Armstrong, *Fields of Blood: Religion and the History of Violence* (Anchor
Books, 2014, 2015), 301.
[189] *Ibid.*, 304.

Klux Klan have traditionally been viewed in the context of being reactionary movements responding to specific ethnographic and religious grievances.[190] However, such analyses either discount or fail to consider extreme violence as an expression of the wartime eschatological anxiety that had taken deep hold within some communities. None need look to "less stable" countries when the malaise, despair, and violence Armstrong describes were quite real in the postwar United States.

Elsewhere organized religions experienced a crisis of purpose and membership. In Germany, Lutheranism was profoundly affected by its vocal support of the war. Over four long years, ministers used the pulpit as a venue to spout virulent anti-Allied (particularly anti-British) propaganda. The November 11, 1918 armistice was so sudden and unexpected, it triggered a series of faith crises across the country. Many saw a Church so morally weakened by its militant pro-war stance as to be partially culpable for the deaths of so many young Germans. Devout congregants latched quickly onto any possible explanation that salvaged their faith – hence, according to A. J. Hoover, the ease with which Christian nationalists in Germany embraced the *dolchstoßlegende* – the "Stab in the Back Myth" – that would prove so damning over the ensuing decades. In the coming years, Hoover argues, many disaffected Lutherans, seeking a moral absolute authority in the absence of the old order, would have little qualms over transferring their own morality to National Socialism. "One could develop a case for the thesis that the first 'German Christians' were not the pro-Nazi Protestants of the Third Reich but the religious patriots of the Great War," Hoover writes. "In the main, German Protestant churchmen were just too eager to blend nationalism and Christianity, to harmonize kaiser and Christ."[191]

At the same time, many of the war's survivors took a more harmonious view on how the war intersected with the secular. According to historian Leonard V. Smith, the average Frenchman's commitment to the war, even

[190] Kelly J Baker, *The Gospel According to the Klan: The KKK's Appeal to Protestant America, 1915–1930* (University Press of Kansas, 2011), 18–19.

[191] A.J. Hoover, *God, Germany, and Britain in the Great War: A Study in Clerical Nationalism* (Praeger Publishers, 1989), 120–122, quotes on 135.

after the great bloodlettings of 1916, was at its heart a matter of informed consent to the ideals of the Republic and the legitimacy of its institutions. Unlike its associates in arms, and its enemies, the French nation was prior to April 1917 the sole republic engaged in the war. Where the other nations could and did rely upon autocratic or monarchical propaganda to maintain their participation in the war, French engagement was contingent upon preserving the citizen-soldier's perspective as the guardian of the Third Republic and the values of French identity. Such action prescribed a willing association on the part of the rank and file. The act of consent to the war and the sacrifices it entailed constituted a social contract that realized as fact the concept of the nation at arms.[192]

A similar perspective is offered by Jonathan Ebel in his study of civic religion and the American military. Accordingly the First World War, for all of its disappointment and contradictory place in the public memory, did serve a purpose in that it provided affirmation of a growing tradition of wartime military service as a call to all citizens to embrace the principles and physical manifestation of the nation. Soldiers become surrogates for all Americans, martyrs and saviors of the republic established in line with Christian principles. Or, as Ebel describes: "The resulting narrative describes a nation that has looked upon its soldiers not simply as protectors and preservers of the nation and its ideals, but as incarnations of those ideals – the Word of the nation made flesh – whose willingness to suffer and die brings salvation to an often wayward but nevertheless chosen people."[193] As noted, this perception of American civic religion is at its core a Christianized perspective. This does not infer a fundamentalist literalism to the outlook. Rather it reflects the discourse offered by the framers and their successors since the American Revolution: that America is a place, and that a people, graced by God with their form of government, are judged fit to keep it through their civic traditions of citizen soldiering in times of trial.[194]

---

[192] Leonard V. Smith, *The Embattled Self: French Soldiers' Testimony of the Great War* (Cornell University Press, 2007), 106–109.

[193] Ebel, *G.I. Messiahs*, 2.

[194] *Ibid.*, 7.

Perhaps the answer to the question lies somewhere in between. Clive Field observes, "the war was, if anything, a setback for organized irreligion as much as for organized religion."[195] Obviously the experiences of combat in the trenches and receiving the news of personal loss after battle proved disheartening for some, triggering a crisis of faith that often crumbled beneath the pressure of survival and bereavement. But the war prompted many more to seek out personal support and succor from the comfortable rituals of faith. Even this is difficult to quantify in any single national case study, let alone across the entire scope of the war and its combatants, however. Open criticism of the organized church hierarchies did certainly increase during and after the war, as the established mainstream churches were held just as accountable as the governments that managed the four-year bloodletting. But interest in the more abstract notion of "spirituality" and independently asserted faith, free of the intrusion and structure imposed by a hierarchical church, grew stronger during the war and remained quite impressive after the war as well. Religion may have been damaged by the war. Faith, and religiosity, thrived.

[195] Clive Field, Keeping the Spiritual Home Fires Burning: Religious Belonging in Britain during the First World War," *War and Society*. 33:4 (October 2014), 244–268, here 267.

Cambridge Elements ≡

Religion and Violence

James R. Lewis
University of Tromsø

James R. Lewis is Professor of Religious Studies at the
University of Tromsø, Norway and the author and editor of a
number of volumes, including *The Cambridge Companion to
Religion and Terrorism*.

Margo Kitts
Hawai'i Pacific University

Margo Kitts edits the *Journal of Religion and Violence* and is
Professor and Coordinator of Religious Studies and East-West
Classical Studies at Hawai'i Pacific University in Honolulu.

ABOUT THE SERIES

Violence motivated by religious beliefs has become all too
common in the years since the 9/11 attacks. Not surprisingly,
interest in the topic of religion and violence has grown sub-
stantially since then. This Elements series on Religion and
Violence addresses this new, frontier topic in a series of ca. fifty
individual Elements. Collectively, the volumes will examine a
range of topics, including violence in major world religious
traditions, theories of religion and violence, holy war, witch
hunting, and human sacrifice, among others.

Cambridge Elements ⁼

Religion and Violence

Transforming the Sacred into Saintliness: Reflecting on Violence and Religion with René Girard
Wolfgang Palaver

Great War, Religious Dimensions
Bobby Wintermute

A full series listing is available at: www.cambridge.org/ERAV

Printed in the United States
By Bookmasters